POTTY TRAININ

GIRLS IN 48 HOURS

A GUIDE FOR MOMS TO POTTY TRAIN THEIR BABY GIRL AND GET HER DIAPER-FREE IN JUST 48 HOURS WITHOUT STRESS. BONUS CHAPTER WITH 21 SPECIAL TIPS FOR YOUR BABY GIRL

Katherine Vinson

TABLE OF CONTENTS:

INTRODUCTION

There is no actual training age. However, the average age most parents begin potty training their girls is between two and three. If your daughter has older siblings, she may learn much earlier than a firstborn.

Whichever the case, you should plan your training wisely, specifically opting for the time when no significant changes are happening in your child's environment. If there are substantial changes in the household, wait until she settles down and no longer feels overwhelmed, then begin the training.

If she is at the stage where she says "no" to everything you ask of her, including potty training, remind yourself that she is only in a phase and that once she is through with it, she will be receptive to new things. You ought to delay the potty training until the stage is over.

Potty Training Equipment

The first step here is to purchase the potty chair or the potty seat and ensure that the child knows that it is hers. This should happen once you notice the signs of readiness, although the training will begin weeks, if not months after. Give the child a chance to interact with the potty and learn how it is used. Encourage your child to personalize the potty by writing her name on it or placing some sparkly stickers.

Your baby will likely feel more at ease training on a potty chair than using the toilet seat right away. You see, children have a natural fear of falling, and since the toilet is raised high above the ground, the child will fear to fall to the side, falling on the steps, or falling into the water when seated. It doesn't help that some seats fidget and do not stick firmly to the big chair.

Everything that a child use must be children-friendly. It should be safe, comfortable, and fun. A good potty chair is one that your child can sit on comfortably, move around the house, and sit or rise from it with ease. Besides the comfort and security, a potty chair is advantageous because the child can use it outside of the bathroom, and the parent can empty the contents in the toilet.

Since there are some excellent potty-training seats in the market, if your child is not afraid, get her one, and ensure that you make the experience as easy for her as you can. Ensure that the seat is secure, comfy, attaches firmly, and does not pinch. Get a step stool to make it easier to get to the top of the toilet bowl.

Ensure that you also stock a variety of fun things your daughter can enjoy while using the potty. Stock some picture manuscripts, or you could download a potty-training app for your child to entertain your daughter as she eases herself.

How to Start Potty Training?

The best learning avenue for children is via imitation. It is easier for them to do what you do than to follow instructions with your mouth. You may spend a lot of time explaining the potty procedure, and your child won't understand what is happening, but if you demonstrate it, she will understand and begin to copy what you do in no time. Therefore, do not close the door when you go in to use the toilet. Leave it open and allow your child to see how it is done.

If daddy does the same and does not lock the bathroom door, your child will make a clear distinction that daddy pees standing up while mummy pees seated. When this happens, take this opportunity to explain the mechanics behind boys peeing standing up and girls doing it while seated. Tell her that girls and their mommies have to pee sitting.

If she needs a little help, demonstrate how it is done using her favorite stuffed animal or doll. Hopefully, she will realize that using the potty is familiar and relatively comfortable.

If, despite your calm efforts, your daughter still will not sit on the potty, avoid pressuring her because that will be the beginning of the power struggle that will derail the training process further.

How to Motivate Her to Use the Potty

The way to get your daughter all excited about potty training is by taking her on a memorable trip to the department store to buy her potty and knickers. Get her some knickers with exceptional designs and her favorite cartoon characters. Also, ensure that the knickers are comfortable to ensure that your child will enjoy wearing them.

Personalize the potty or seat also by allowing her to decorate it with some stickers or writing on its sides with some glitter glue. She could use the glue to make interesting patterns. After this, have her sit on the chair with clothes on for practice. Doing these things should get your child excited about becoming a big girl who can now use grown-up stuff.

The way to build up the excitement is to plan the trip. Get her talking about it every day, and when she does something right around the house or behaves well, let her know that you will give her a reward when you take her to buy some "big girl stuff" like the potty and the knickers. Tell her that once you begin the training, she will start to be like her elder sisters or like mommy. Keep the hope and excitement alive so that when you finally make the trip, your child will be more than excited about purchasing and using the potty-training stuff.

When to Banish Nappies

A child will learn and stick with any skill, so long as it is presented in her environment consistently. If potty training is made a consistent plan so that the parent, nanny, and the caregiver at the daycare are a coordinated team who uses the same potty-training approach, your child will learn the skill much quicker.

The best approach to training is to switch from using diapers to underwear all day, from the very beginning. This way, there will be no switching methods in the middle of the training, and your child will not be confused. You could also take up the use of pull-up training pants. Still, experts agree that it is the washable cotton training pants that produce the best experience because your daughter will be conscious of her wetness immediately when an accident happens. Be prepared that there will be several accidents before the child fully masters the use of the potty.

Whenever you are out, carry with you some clean knickers, pair of tights, and some trousers, even when you are only taking a short trip to the store. If you leave your child at a daycare or preschool when you go to work during the day, ensure that you leave a more massive stack of the items your daughter could need during the day. When you leave your child under the care of a nanny or a sitter, ensure that they have quick access to the extra clothes. If you need advice and tips on carrying on the training stress-free, talk to other moms in your playgroup to find out how they solve some of the challenges they encounter. Remember, though, that every child is different and requires a unique approach. Whenever you want to try something new, talk to your child's pediatrician first.

Weeing, Pooping, And Preventing Infection

For girls, even wiping takes a specific strategy. Teach her that she ought to wipe from the front to the back whenever she uses the potty, especially if she had a poo. This is a healthy practice that keeps bacteria from the bowel spreading into the areas of the vagina and the urethra. If she has difficulty stretching her hand to effectively wipe front to back, opt that she pats herself dry after peeing, and when she poops, she should call for assistance to wipe.

It is not uncommon to see a case of a urinary tract infection (UTI) in a child, especially girls. The illness develops when the child holds in urine for too long, and when bowel bacteria get to the vagina and proceed to the urethra.

UTIs in children are identified through the following signs. The first is that the child will begin to complain of some pain whenever she pees or some discomfort around the pelvis or tummy region. The second sign is that all of a sudden, the girl will begin to wet her pants, even after successful potty training and having achieved reasonable bladder control. The third sign is that the child will develop a need to pee more often, and usually, the extreme urge to pee comes suddenly. If you notice any of these signs in your child, rush her to a hospital to have her treated.

How Can She Recognize the Signs of Needing A Wee?

Your little girl will have to learn how to tell when she needs to go to the potty by herself. You may keep reminding her at the beginning of the training, but with time, she will have to be sensitive enough to know when she needs a wee. The way to cultivate this sensitivity is to have your child spend some considerable time during the day without any underwear. This is so that when the pee comes gushing out, the child will feel and see it flow so that whenever the feeling comes, she will associate it with wetness, and she will rush to find the potty.

The potty should always be within your child's reach. Ensure that the distance between the potty and the area from which the child is playing is short to get to it in time. With that said, be ready for the occasional puddles when the child is unable to get to the potty and when she is unable to sit on the potty chair properly, resulting in some liquid drops to the floor.

Have some cleaning agents, such as a carpet cleaner, at hand, or you could cover your carpet with some plastic to keep it from absorbing the fluids.

When to Praise Her During Potty Training

Children love to know that they have their parents' support and approval in all they do. They like to make their parents proud and receive recognition and praise in exchange. Your little girl is like that. She wants to know that she is making you happy and proud as she learns how to use the potty. Praise will also tell her that she is getting into the "big girl" league, just like mom and the elder sisters. This will be a dream come true for her because toddlers like to think of themselves as adults, equal to their mothers and other older people in the house.

When your daughter eventually gets something in her potty, celebrate this tremendous success. Shower her with praise, telling her how confident she was, how happy she looked, and how grown-up her actions were. Reward her, possibly a sticker of her favorite cartoon character, her favorite food, a cookie, some juice, and your child fancies. If she loves bedtime stories, promise to read her an extra one as she goes to bed at night, and ensure that you keep your promise.

CHAPTER 1: IS IT TIME FOR POTTY TRAINING?

Children cannot control their bladder or bowel movements before the age of 12 months. Some children who display several signs of preparation are still unable to control their removal physically. But kids who can stay dry overnight can take longer to stay dry overnight. Indeed, you may want to think of day and night dryness as two different milestones for potty training.

You don't have to wait for every element to start training. Only look for an independence pattern and an understanding of what it means to be in the bathroom like an adult. To help you get started, read the positive potty-training techniques.

The effectiveness of potty training depends more on preparation than on your child's age.

Visual signals are often synchronized to walk and even to run.

She urinates at one time a decent volume and has frequent, well-formed bowel movements at predictable intervals.

She has "dry" intervals of 2 hours or more or during naps, indicating that her bladder muscles are adequately formed to retain urine.

Behavioral Symptoms

- Can sit quietly for 2-5 minutes in one spot.
- Could pull up and down her pants.
- Dislikes a wet or dirty diaper feeling.
- Shows a curiosity in others' behaviors (would like to watch or wear underwear to go to the bathroom).
- Give a physical or verbal indication if she has a bowel movement like grunting, sputtering, or asking you.
- It indicates a desire for freedom.
- She takes pride in her achievements.

- It's not difficult to learn to use the bathroom.
- It is not harmful or contrary at a generally cooperative level.
- Cognitive signs
- Recognize the physical signals, which means that she needs to go and warn you before it happens, or even hold it until she has time for the potty.
- Can obey basic directions, like "go get the toy."
- Understand how important it is to place items where they belong.
- Has urine and stool names.

10 Indicators of Potty Readiness

Until your kid is ready to start, other indicators of readiness for potty training include:

1. They have fewer wet diapers: If your kid's painting has been planned regularly and is only ready every few hours to turn to the toilet. This is a sign that they begin to regulate, which is vital for the handling of the bladder.
2. Their bowel movements are predictable—a kid who pulls in time off the potty before anything happens. If you know that your child is always about 8 a.m., you know you're ready with the toilet. It raises the probability of proper potty training.
3. They are their body shop. How do you think you have to go? How do you feel you have to go? Your body tells you! Your body tells you! Children who can listen to their bodies are better suited for the potty than children whose desires and distress are ignored. A child with a body sensitivity will grunt, squat, or cover from pseudo-privacy under a table.
4. The use of the toilet requires more flexibility than the use of a diaper. Children must, first of all, be able to remove their clothing. They're potty prepared if your kid can do this.
5. They understand directions. Most kids think they don't know what's going on. It never really changes for children–adolescents

too! But it's time for your kid to take the diapers if it can follow clear instructions –stuff like "go potty" and "sit down."

6. They will sit for several minutes. Make sure they will stay quiet before putting your child in the toilet. You don't want your child to use the pot when they get up and open the midpoop door.

7. When your child runs around the house, singing, "I'm always baby here, I roar!" They want freedom, you know. Girls who want to establish themselves as heads of households are more likely than girls to attend toilet training.

8. They complain about being wet. They're ready for underwear if you have one kid who doesn't like wet in a wall.

9. They're curious about the bathroom. If the child asks questions about the toilet–where toilet paper goes when they're flushed, why do people go, be it moms or daddy picks and dumbbells? Girls tend to be like their parents, and they'll want to be like that when they see you out of diapers (hopefully you are!).

10. They tell you they want to go. Maybe the sure sign that your little girl is ready to use the toilet is most natural. When children learn how to communicate their wishes, let them loose, and fulfill their porcelain dreams.

CHAPTER 2: YOUR CHILD'S PREPAREDNESS

Your child's preparedness is the primary factor to consider; however, some other suggestions we have as far as the time frame you should think of for toilet training.

By and large, it would be best if you attempted this gigantic undertaking when there are little questions and minimal movement. Potty preparing around Christmas or Thanksgiving can be diverting. You have to commit a great deal of consideration regarding your baby, and with a ton going on all through the excursions, you likely won't do that.

Nevertheless, if you have a long holiday weekend without needing to fret about work, working on potty training throughout this time could be a great time to start.

Make potty training a leading priority consistently when you have the emotional and physical energy to do it. Even if your kid reveals signs of potty-training preparedness, you may not be ready for it as a mom and dad.

Clear your timetable and be prepared for anything! Select an opportunity to start the potty preparing when your family's standard is most drastically averse to be disturbed with home guests, occasions from the house, a migration, etc. Guarantee you're not pre-busy with other giant duties, for example, work, either.

You might want to get out a calendar and talk with your child about a great time to begin extensive potty training. Ask your child when s/he wishes to start to learn how to use the potty. Circle the date in a bright color and keep advising her that "potty day" is almost here.

Different not exactly ideal occasions to begin potty preparing are during unpleasant circumstances, for example, when going on an outing, around the hour of a birth of a sibling or sister, or when making another enormous life change for your child, for example, taking out the container or transforming from a den to a bed.

Take these elements into consideration when you prepare to introduce toilet teaching. It may be better to postpone it until your kid's environment is stable and safe.

Also, though some experts might recommend beginning the process throughout summertime because children wear less clothing, it is not an excellent idea to wait to start if your child is ready.

Typically, training your little youngster to utilize the potty isn't a short-term understanding. The method ordinarily takes somewhere in the range of 3 and a half years, even though it may require some investment for specific children.

And although some youngsters can discover to both make it through the night without moistening or staining themselves (or the bed) and use the potty around the same time, it might take an extra six months to 1 year to master remaining dry the evening.

There are some people out there who will offer "systems" that can assist you in teaching your child to utilize the potty within 48-hours-- or perhaps less. They may help, but potty training is a lengthy learning procedure that takes total dedication.

Kids can encounter strain as well. They are attempting to potty train while your kid is under a specific amount of worry for whatever factor can be irritating for both of you. Evade this extensive advance during conditions such as this.

Latrine preparation is a learning strategy, not a disciplinary cycle, and a mind-boggling one at that! Your child needs to comprehend what you need and afterward needs to find how to do it. Notwithstanding understanding the physical encounters, getting to the restroom, and getting garments off, a child needs to tighten sphincter muscles to achieve control at first, and afterward loosen up them to take out.

There is a long way to go. Getting entrail and bladder control is a capacity, and luckily, kids usually prefer to discover shiny new abilities.

The capability of capacities regularly follows an example. First is gut consistency, commonly followed by entrail control. Daytime bladder control naturally comes after. However, for various kids, this can coincide, and finally, after (regularly much soon) comes evening bladder control.

Also, a few youngsters accomplish daytime and evening control simultaneously. With the swing towards a more direct technique to latrine preparing from the past age, kids will, in general, be prepared after, and all the more frequently, their entrail and bladder capacities go under their control simultaneously.

Some parents choose to take a more easygoing method for toilet training. They let the child go when they wish to, and if they have a mishap, they gloss over it with little referral. For some individuals, this can work, but it's bound to take a lot longer than standard toilet training.

If you do choose a passive, more laissez-faire mindset about toilet training, remember that children still need to understand what it is that is anticipated of them. You are not always "pushing" your kid by supplying direction and expectations. Some children are ready to be trained early, so you are not "pressing" if you are meeting no resistance. Let their resistance be your guide. Children do love finding out full-grown behavior, so accept them their opportunity if it fits their preparedness.

So, existing ways you can assist along with the procedure? You wager!

CHAPTER 3: DEMYSTIFYING MYTHS AND MISCONCEPTION

As a parent, you probably love celebrating your child's "first milestones," so it's all about the first food they had, their first steps, first words, their first year, and, of course, their first time going to the potty!

But why do we, as caregivers, get excited about pooping and peeing in the potty? Well, think about it, before a toddler is potty trained, you probably spent a considerable amount of money on diapers! We love our children, there's no doubt about it, but we also need to protect our wallets!

And, most importantly, have you seen how much a toddler eats?! Some of those diapers are unbelievable and out of this world! So, yes, we need to get excited and happy once our toddlers start using the potty.

But not everybody thinks this way. There are some myths and misconceptions that have been flying around... faster than your toddler! And now I am going to take my time to debunk them because, in all honesty, they are all pretty poop. I mean, they are not based on scientific research!

Continue reading and see for yourself how grown-ups have spread these myths about potty training.

Children Should Tell Their Parents When They Are Ready to Potty Train.

I genuinely wish this was true; this way, we would save so much time, and, instead of worrying, we would be able to sleep throughout the night! Because, trust me, when my toddler was potty training, I used to go to bed, and all I was able to think about was my toddler peeing and pooping throughout the house. I would even spend hours online searching for methods to clean a white sofa, because, guess what? Uhm, sofas are a great potty.

So, can you imagine your toddler telling you they are ready to potty train? "Mom, Dad, I am now a big girl, and I'm ready to break up with those horrible diapers and go potty train with you. Bring it on, parents!".

All jokes aside, no, this myth is a myth for a reason, and it wouldn't work in real life. We need to wait for our children to give us some cues when physically, mentally, and psychologically ready, but they won't even know they are willing to potty train until we empower them to do so!

Make Your Child Sit on The Potty, And That's It.

Again, I genuinely wish things were so simple! Potty training is not about sitting your child on the potty and voilà - they have learned it in five minutes.

There is more to it than this. Potty training is all about practicing doing something, and even if they know how to do pee and poop (because we know they know!), the fact that they need to sit on something, and the fact that they are not wearing diapers is all too much for them.

They may go to the potty if you sit them, because, wow! New experiences alert! They will probably pee once or twice; however, they won't be potty trained yet.

My Child's Daycare Will Probably Train Them There.

Oh, no. I'm so sorry to burst this bubble for you. I am. The truth is, no, they won't. Many daycares will even turn away parents who haven't potty trained their children yet because they are aware of the enormous responsibility behind this milestone.

You could start potty training, and then you could have a chat with whoever is in charge of the daycare and see whether they could support your potty-training journey. Few daycares will do this.

And it all makes sense if you think about it. First of all, they probably have many children around the same age, who are likely to be on a potty-training journey. Can you imagine if they have to teach all of them how to use the bathroom? They are going to be inside the toilet for the whole day!

Second, they don't know your child yet, and they don't know how you are potty training at home. And this is a huge responsibility to take on, so are you sure you would like to give it away to someone else?

Pull-Up Style Training Pants Are Simply the Best for Training.

Well, it could be. Or you could be swapping one thing for the other one! Pull-up pants are diapers, albeit cheaper. Most toddlers will simply make a new association between needing the potty and the pull-up pant. So, you will end up cleaning those pants instead!

All Children Must Be Potty Trained as Soon as They Turn 2.

Again, who said this!? Every child is different, saying this makes parents feel confused because what if their child is not ready? Does it mean they are falling behind? Do they have a developmental problem? Well, no, not at all.

Putting all children in the same category is, if I'm honest, quite irresponsible. We should take the pressure off of the milestones. Your child will give you the signals when she is ready. How many 9-year-olds have you seen wearing a diaper? Exactly!

Children Are Potty Trained Very Quickly.

I am guilty of this one. I thought all children would learn to use the potty very rapidly, because, after all, they already know how to pee and poop, so, they are already 90% there? Ha! I was so wrong.

Not only did this myth shake me, but it also made me realize that making a comparison with other children is not healthy! Again, every child will learn differently. Some will take 2, 3, 4 days, whereas others can take up to a year. And guess what? They have all learned the same skill so that I wouldn't worry about this.

Potty Training Is A Great Opportunity to Bond with Your Child.

Awesome. It's also an excellent opportunity to learn about the different types of poop my toddler can produce. It sounds impressive.

All parents will go through this, I know it, but you need to be extra patient not to lose it. You need to laugh about the accidents because otherwise, your child will feel you are tense. You need to expect the worst and kind of hope for the best, knowing that this phase will pass.

I'm 100% confident that I wouldn't use the word "bonding." However, as an adult, I would probably bond with my mum because I am now aware of what she had to do to get me on that potty. But, connecting with my toddler over potty training? I'm not sure. she wasn't interested either. she was just happy to play around with water when it was finally time to wash her hands.

Once A Toddler Is Potty Trained, They Are Potty Trained Forever.

I think this myth was created by someone who wasn't a parent! I mean, have they ever heard of diarrhea? Colics? Television? Because all of those things don't let your child get to the potty quick enough!

Accidents are bound to happen, especially when they are still in the early stages of potty training. Besides, sure, you need to be consistent with potty training. Still, there are so many situations that could make your child have a setback—for example, the arrival of a new baby or a difficult situation at home.

So, no, toddlers who are potty trained could go back to diapers in no time.

Toddlers Need to Be Disciplined When They Are Potty Training.

If, by disciplined, you mean, you should punish them or do something to let them know who is in charge, then no, you shouldn't be turning potty training into a power struggle. This is not what it is about.

You shouldn't lie to your children about not having more diapers, you shouldn't bribe them to go to the potty, and you should not threaten your child if they don't use the potty or if they have an accident.

This behavior will only end with a toddler who has anxiety issues, fear, and even self-esteem problems.

Children Should Be Potty Trained for Day and Night at The Same Time.

Another false myth. The reality is that these two pieces of training occur during different stages. Nighttime potty training is often associated with hormones and urine production. Unless you are willing to change their clothes and sheets every night for an unknown period, I would suggest you wait until your toddler has thoroughly potty trained during the day. Then you will be able to potty train them at night.

This approach (where a toddler is potty trained both at day and night) could be correct for some families, but overall, it is a myth.

CHAPTER 4: BEING MENTALLY PREPARED

Therefore, you want to train your baby with the potty, but you don't know where to look because you've never done it before. Well, you're in the right place. I'll show you some fantastic training resources to go to the toilet. I will give you the basics here. First of all, potty training is not only about technique but also about mentality. You see that many people think they are just technical and end up spending a lot of time spinning the wheels in an attempt to make their baby go to the toilet frequently.

Look, no matter what technique or method you use to train to go to the toilet, it doesn't matter if you want your child to teach standing or sitting, you should remember that mentality is everything. Let's go deeper and see what these mentalities are. It must be consistent with your child's potty training. Sometimes you have to do your best and tell your babysitter or anyone who takes care of your child to train as insignificantly as you do. If it is inconsistent, this can send mixed messages to your child, and the results will be unstable. This implies that, if you want your child to pass the urinal to urinate and defecate continuously, it must be consistent with the potty training.

Motivational training can be a frustrating test for you and your child if you let them do it. Therefore, you must understand that your child is a child and let her do it if she is wrong. You don't have to show your child that you are disappointed in her but show that you are dissatisfied with the disaster it caused. You can do this by disapproving faces and statements by cleaning up the mess. Don't worry if your child understands if she still doesn't speak the language. Most of the communication takes place through body language, and the child will receive the message. Children of this age naturally want to please their parents, so use it in their favor.

In addition to showing your disapproval for cleaning up the mess, you shouldn't show signs of disapproval during the whole mundane training process. This is always the source of a positive reinforcement mentality. Don't scold anything during training. It is frustrating for you and your baby. Your baby is capable of extraordinary things but not without errors because, after all, we are all human beings. Be positive and look at your child in amazement by quickly learning what to do.

By adhering to the positive mindset, you should reward your child for doing the right thing, urinating, defecating in the toilet, or any other training potty she chooses. You can have a snack, preferably salty, as your child will want to drink more water so that your child has more opportunities to practice. You can also use the training tables to reward. Soon I will publish one of these on my blog, so check my blog frequently.

You can train your baby in just 48-hours with the right method if you fully commit. This implies that you may need to take a few days off from work or that your child needs to take a few days off from kindergarten. Commit yourself and your time to remain constant during training, and you will see how your child will return your consistency and commitment to the results.

CHAPTER 5: LETTING GO OF THE DIAPERS! WHERE DO WE START?

We are potty training, so we will have to get rid of those diapers. Day one was spent naked, so we didn't need an alternative, but day two could be spent on clothing. That means you may want to introduce underwear. Some parents are okay with putting their child in training pants during potty training and for a while after, and others swear by putting them straight into underwear. What you choose will much depend on you and your child.

Your child has developed the muscle memory to their diaper. They have been in that diaper since the day they were born. They are used to having it at their disposal, and they feel safe with it on. They have now spent two to three years in peeing and pooping in their diaper when it comes to potty training. But, guess what also feels like a snug-feeling diaper.

Underwear.

That's why parents who end up transitioning too quickly will experience a whole lot of accidents. The kid doesn't understand that underwear is different than their diapers. For a child, their underwear's snug feeling is similar enough to wear a diaper that it is pretty much an automatic response. This is especially true when it comes to poop.

With all that said, there are clues to look for in your child and a transition that you can try to make their transition into underwear easier.

How Well Are They Potting?

Your child may be using the potty reasonably well, but is it mostly at your request? Do they tell you to go, or are you still taking them every few minutes or hours? It is best to wait until they have started to let you know when they need to go because that means they have learned how to recognize the urges in their own body. You may experience something that not many parents experience. Some children will refuse to wear diapers anymore, for whatever reason, and that would be your biggest clue that they are ready for the transition into underwear.

Pull-Ups, Training Pants, Or Underwear

Most people have some pretty strong opinions about what toddlers need to wear when they are potty trained. What it boils down to is that you have to decide what will be best for your child. Whether or not you should use pull-ups or other disposable training pants will depend on your child's age, personality, and situation, and how well you can manage accidents. You likely won't know which is going to be the best option until you get into the thick of it. However, there are some things you can consider.

Training Pants

While your child may use the potty and is happy to oblige you when you ask them to, they may still be too young to have complete control over their bladder functions. This could cause them to get upset when they accidentally wet themselves. Pull-ups or washable training pants could be a good idea to start with.

They are good to use because:

- They can help them get through the night
- They prevent messes when accidents happen
- They can boost motivation in some
- They provide your kid with a "big kid" feel
- They are a better option for toddlers who don't have full bladder control

They aren't a good option because:

- Disposable training pants can become costly

- They will sometimes diminish motivation in toddlers
- They promote sitting in wetness just like a diaper

Though, training pants are a clear step up from them wearing diapers, and most toddlers like the sound of being a "big" kid. While disposable training pants can end up being a crutch for some, since they are a lot like diapers, if your child is already motivated to be potty trained, they likely won't be. They will be a safety tool that can keep your child from getting upset with themself for making a mess.

They will also prevent any big messes that you may have to clean up around the house during the training process until your child gets pottying.

That said, there are washable training pants, as mentioned earlier. They help protect from messes and have all the benefits of pull-ups, but they also allow your child to wear underwear. They are waterproof underwear that goes over the top of their regular underwear. If they have an accident, all you have to do is wash them, which can be done in the washer or by hand. They dry quickly so that you can reuse them more often.

Underwear

Since most children aren't ready to start training until after two years of age, they may be prepared to jump right into underwear. These older children also tend to be hard to get motivated for potty training because they have a more assertive independence streak, and praise and reward charts might not work well. That also means that pull-ups are likely the wrong decision, at least when it comes to daytime training.

This is where cloth training pants that will absorb part of the wetness and then transition into regular underwear could be a better option. When they have an accident in thing cotton underwear, the only choice is to stop playing and get cleaned up. This alone is typically enough to motivate the otherwise engaged child to notice all of the signs needed to get to the bathroom.

Regular Underwear May Be the Best Choice for Your Child If:

- Your toddler seems to need a push. If you are positive that they are developmentally ready to be toilet trained, but they aren't interested in giving up the convenience of using their diaper, introducing them to underwear that is exciting to them, think superheroes, and requires them to use the toilet if they want to keep them can be the best motivator.

- Having to deal with messes isn't a big deal to you. Accidents will often upset a sensitive child, so you may want to think about choosing something that has a little more absorbency if your child is easily upset by accidents. You also have to make sure that you are free to clean up any accidents that will likely happen when you first start training.

- Your toddler tells you that they need to use the bathroom or go on their own, and they don't require constant prompting and reminding.

One last thing you should think about when choosing between pull-ups and underwear is cost. Pull-ups and other such brands will end up costing more than regular diapers, so they are a lot more expensive than a couple of packs of cotton underwear.

Now, after dealing with potty training for one day, you have likely learned what type of potty trainer they are going to be like. To help you transition into underwear, we will look at the five main types of trainers and handle them.

The Puppy

These trainers are the ones that feel confident, and they will often make it on their own to the potty before they poop or pee. They are the ones that are the readiest for underwear and will make the transition more positively if they continue to feel that Mom and Dad are respecting their potty-training timetable.

They like to find out that they are using the potty the right way, and it may take some time until they feel as if they are in control.

You have to make sure that they have the chance to take part in the underwear picking process. The time that you spend with them picking out their underwear is a bonding time. The emotional connection you can form with them at this point is going to be helpful after stages in their life. Let them pick out where they will keep their new underwear.

When the time comes that they do have an accident in their new underwear, the calmer and more relaxed you can be responding to this, the better. This will help to keep your little one calm as well.

The Turtle

These kids are the ones who don't do too well when being introduced to a new routine. If they get moved into something new too quickly can create a setback. You will want to wait until they show more confidence before you try to get them into underwear. They will likely take better to wearing pull-ups since they are similar to diapers.

You can take them shopping to see if she finds any that she likes, but you shouldn't be too surprised if they end up feeling too overwhelmed.

When they do pick out some, or if you buy some on your own, place them after their pull-ups. It would be best if you made sure that their routine stays as close to normal as possible to remain comfortable. Check-in with them from time to time to see if they are ready to make the transition.

The Owl

This child likes to see their options. They will likely be doing pretty good at keeping their diaper or pull-ups dry and goes the bathroom with confidence. You can then introduce them to underwear. Explain to them what the differences are between them. Show them side by side. Let them know that they are worn the same way and that you pull them up and down. They will pick up fairly quickly and likely show an interest in taking the following steps in potty training.

This child will also want to be involved in the entire process of getting underwear and will want to pick out their own.

The Squirrel

These kiddos don't have time to waste on focusing on what you are saying. Once they have shown that they can focus long enough to use the potty when they need to, you can introduce them to big kid underwear. They will either want to help you shop, or they won't be able to focus on helping you shop. Either way, make sure you get them plenty of styles, colors, and designs to keep them interested.

They may love the idea of showing off their new undies in a bedroom fashion show. For them, it may be a good idea to place a small, lined hamper in the bathroom that gets used for nothing but their wet underwear. They will likely be the one that swoops in and out of the bathroom doing their business without you realizing it, so you want to have everything ready for them when needed.

The Bear Cub

This child is very independent and probably won't be as excited for underwear as the others. This is because they probably prefer the idea of filling up their diaper or Pull-Ups is better than interrupting their playtime to go to the bathroom. Don't worry, though; they will become interested in underwear.

An excellent way to introduce them to underwear is to sneak some into their clothes to see them when they get dressed in the morning. There is a good chance that the lingerie they find may end up on their head or their teddy bear, but that is okay. This will help to cultivate some interest.

CHAPTER 6: NIGHTTIME TRAINING PATTERN

The truth is there isn't much for you to teach here. We sleep at night, and we are not consciously able to control our bodies. Instead, our unconscious mind takes over complete control. This is super important to understand, so let me say it another way. At night time, when a person is sleeping, she can't consciously evaluate what she does or does not do. There are a lot of unconscious processes happening in our bodies at all times. Our hearts beat. We breathe. We produce waste. We digest food and fight viruses and bacteria. Our hair grows. Our cuts heal. Every single one of these processes is unconscious. It's a good thing too! Can you imagine trying to keep track of all that stuff consciously?

Holding in our pee is unconscious, too, especially at night. But even in the daytime, holding in pee is out as well, up to a point. It only becomes a conscious process when your bladder is full enough to signal your conscious mind to take care of business. But at night time, that signal has to wake you up first. This is a learned skill.

The bad news is you can't teach your child how to hold in her pee while sleeping. You can't teach her to wake up when she has a full bladder. The good news is that all healthy children eventually learn this skill. The further right information is that you can motivate a child to learn faster if moving too slowly. When I say "motivate," I do mean encourage and not punish or criticize.

Establishing A Night Time Pattern

I recommend that all parents give their kids a chance to expect some regular patterns in their lives. Patterns are predictable and help kids to know what to expect after. They reduce stress. They induce calmness. I'm not saying you should teach your child to lead a boring life, but when it comes to the regular maintenance aspects of life, patterns are a good thing.

For night time potty training, I suggest you make dinner the last chance to eat for the evening. Nighttime snacking only encourages weight gain anyway, so we parent should adopt the same pattern. Isn't it better to model healthy eating habits now, while the kids are still young? I think so.

If you cut out food consumption after dinner, you'll have an easier time cutting down on liquids as well. Food makes us thirsty. Thirsty kids will ask for water, juice, or milk. They'll nag you until you give in. It's hard to say no because it seems cruel to let a child go to bed thirsty.

If your children need to have something before bed, give them a small quantity of water. If you've ever been on a plane where the airline serves you those tiny portions of juice, usually a 1/2 cup serving, you know what I mean by a small amount. And that's considered small for an adult! For a small child, I suggest you keep a plastic cup in the bathroom and use a minimal amount of water in the cup to let the child have a drink before bed. It's just enough to wet her mouth and keep her comfortable.

Caution: I'm not suggesting you deny your proper child hydration. The above recommendation does not apply if your child has diarrhea or any other condition that causes dehydration. Use common sense!

The few suggestions relate to making night time accidents less stressful and less of a problem for you and your child. Using these tips, you'll be in a much better state of mind to stay calm when accidents happen. And they will happen.

Put the Potty in The Bedroom

One tip that worked wonderfully in my house is to put the potty in your child's room at night. If possible, place it in a well-lit corner of the room, beside the night light.

When tuck-in time is finished, your child will lie in bed and drift off to sleep. But sometimes we don't go to sleep right away, right? Our minds need to calm down first, and it might take 30 minutes or even an hour to fall asleep. During that time, the body is producing urine. Because the potty is right there in the child's room, she may get up to go pee again, on her own, and in the comfort of her room, before falling asleep.

If you are worried about pee dripping on the carpet, put an old towel under the potty. If you're concerned about germs and handwashing, put a box of bum wipes beside the potty and teach your child to use them to clean her hands.

Using this technique with our two girls was highly effective. Only once did we have a small problem, where our daughter was excited to dump her pee in the toilet the following morning. She spilled the pee on her carpet. I got down to business with a wet-dry vacuum and sucked it up as best as I could. I then re-wet the carpet with fresh water and vacuumed that up too. I repeated these 5 or 6 times to dilute any remaining pee in the carpet.

Protect the Mattress

It might take a while to complete night time potty training, but it only takes one big pee to soak into a mattress rendering it smelly forever. So, use protection. Wrap that mattress in a waterproof cover.

You can buy these at any bedding or big box retail store. Some planning will save you money, such as shopping online. My advice is don't believe the cheapest cover. You can buy covers for under $15, but be sure to read the reviews. If you go to Amazon, always look to see what the authors of 1-star ratings have complained about.

Here's an example. I browsed Amazon to find a seemingly good quality mattress cover under $20. I found one for $12 that sounded amazing based on the description. Better yet, of the 97 reviews, 57 of them were rated five stars. But, as soon as I read the 13 studies that gave it a 1-star rating, it became clear that this product is not waterproof as claimed. Nearly every 1-star review said the same thing. They all read something like this: "My daughter has accidents, and I thought this was waterproof. It's not. All the liquid soaked right through to the mattress". If you have to spend an extra few buck to save a mattress, it's smart insurance.

In our house, we always relied on the PVC mattress covers that zip over the entire mattress. We bought them at Walmart, but you can get them pretty much anywhere. They're cheap enough, and you know they are waterproof. Yes, they wrinkle a bit when your child rolls around, but it doesn't matter. Your child's bedding will all go on top of this mattress protector.

Protect the Sheets

Protecting the mattress is just smart long-term thinking. But watching the sheets is about reducing short term hassles. When your child inevitably wets the bed, you want to contain the pee as much as possible. There isn't anything you can do about pee-soaked pajamas, but you can minimize wetness to the bedsheets in most cases. If there is a bit of pee on the sheets, it won't hurt anyone. What we're trying to do here is save you work. We don't want you to have to wash sheets every day.

The best protection is to use a pad on top of the main fitted sheet. Your child will lie directly on this pad, with the bedsheets over top of her. When she has an accident, most of the pee will end up being absorbed into the pillow.

If the pad isn't comfortable enough, or if you simply don't have one, you can use big beach towels to protect the sheets as well. To do this, take a large beach towel and lay it so that the long side of the towel lays across the short side of the bed. This way, you'll have enough length to tuck the towel into the sides of the bed. Again, the towel should go right on top of the fitted sheet, with all other bedding on top.

Put your child to bed as per usual. Kiss her good night and go about enjoying the rest of your evening. Then, just before you go to bed, sneak into your child's room and try your best to adjust the cover sheets, so they aren't trapped beneath your child. Sheets that are under your child are in the danger zone of being peed on. Then go to bed.

Dealing with Accidents: A Little Preparation Goes A Long Way.

Inevitably, when an accident happens, your child will start whining or crying, or he'll come over to you and wake you up. You'll notice her soaked pajamas. You'll walk over to her bedroom and grab her a fresh pair. You'll rip off the towels or mattress pad, exposing clean and dry sheets. Put your child back to bed and toss the towels in the laundry bin. Deal with those tomorrows. For now, it's back to sleep for everyone. This whole routine shouldn't take more than 2 or 3 minutes to deal with.

As time goes on, teach your child how to deal with these accidents on her own. Most toddlers can take off their wet pajama pants and even put on a new, dry pair. They can learn how to take the damp bed pad off the bed and sleep on the clean, dry sheet underneath it.

If you train your child to deal with most of her accidents, you will find that you either don't get disturbed at all, or the disturbance is short, and everyone goes back to bed quickly. Kids who wake up soaking wet don't enjoy it. They don't want to be awake. They often fall back asleep very quickly. So just help solve the problem and get everyone back in bed (including you).

Bedwetting Privacy: Understand the Embarrassment

When kids wet the bed, they can feel embarrassed. It's completely normal to have this feeling. The child knows she isn't supposed to wet her bed. She knows many of her friends don't wet the bed. So, she's not exactly keen to discuss it openly.

You need to keep your child's feelings in mind when having conversations about bedwetting around others. It's natural for you to want to chat with your friends or family members about it. But keep in mind that your kids hear what you say when they're around, even if they don't seem to be paying attention.

Avoid talking about bedwetting with anyone when your child is in earshot. It's just not worth the risk of increasing your child's embarrassment. And especially don't speak about it in a way that communicates disappointment. "Oh, I hardly slept last night. I had to get up again to change my girl's sheets because she wet the bed". That kind of language is a thinly veiled attempt at shaming poor girl. It won't help speed up her learning, and it likely causes resentment on her part. You have just given her a reason to pee her bed whenever she's upset with you.

CHAPTER 7: FIRST TIME DRAMA

On the first day, wake up your toddler, or wait until they decide to get up, then take them to the bathroom as soon as they get up. If you happen to catch them before using their diaper, you can start on the right foot and have them use the potty right away. However, don't be disappointed or upset if you don't get to them soon enough. You can move on to the following step.

The second step is to wait twenty minutes. You're going to take your toddler to the bathroom quite often throughout the day. It should be every twenty minutes, which is three times an hour. Take them to the toilet, put them on their training potty, and tell them in a happy voice to go to the bathroom. Make sure you're optimistic! This shouldn't ever be a negative experience for your toddler.

They won't be able to pee every twenty minutes. You're just teaching them to sit on the potty and try to go. They'll be able to go every couple of times, hopefully, or about every hour or two hours.

This might not occur on the first day. The idea is to get them to push and try every time they sit on the potty. They should have gone once or twice by the end of your first day. Even a little bit of pee when they sit down is impressive progress! You're helping them avoid an accident by giving them many chances to use the bathroom.

You don't have to praise them insanely every time they sit on the potty. If they try but don't happen to produce anything, tell them, "Good try." Every time they sit down is helpful in terms of teaching them how to use the bathroom. Save your enthusiastic praise for the actual event. You want them to be excited when you're excited because this gives them the motivation to keep trying to use the bathroom.

When they begin peeing on the floor (and they will), run over to them as soon as you see it happen. Please pick them up and take them to the potty to use it. When you see them beginning to pee on the floor, tell them, "Pee-pee doesn't go on the floor, it goes in the potty!" Do every time. This is the reason you should restrict their space and keep them naked.

Being on the other side of the house, away from the potty, will be challenging to handle when this happens. On the other hand, being only a few steps away from the bathroom will make this process a lot easier, as they'll still be peeing when you get them to the potty. Praise them if they end up getting a few dribbles in the potty. This will reinforce the idea of peeing in the potty.

For example, if you catch your toddler beginning to pee on the floor, pick them up quickly and tell them that pee goes in the potty. Take them a few steps to the potty and sit them down to finish in the training potty. When they finish, that's a success! Cheer and smile; show your toddler the pee in the training potty. Then have them help you carry that to the potty and flush it. Showing them the flushing of their urine reinforces the idea that this is normal.

It's essential to have your toddler wash their hands with you and tell them you're proud of going to the bathroom on the potty. Then go back to the designated area and show them where they went on the floor. Tell them that they don't pee on the floor, it's gross, and that pee goes in the potty. Point to the potty, then clean up the mess. Repeat this for 48-hours. If they don't go again within twenty minutes, take them to the potty and try to go. Repeat every twenty minutes.

Now that you have demonstrated to them what will happen, you must keep it up! That means every twenty minutes for the entire day for 48-hours. They should be naked throughout the day, except for naptime and bedtime. Nighttime potty training is different from daytime potty training.

Consider it a success if your toddler attempts to go to the potty, pees on the potty, or acknowledges that they have had an accident when they have pee running down their legs. This will be the case for most kids, starting around the middle of the first day. Every child will be different; their personalities are different, so the rate at which they learn to go on the potty will differ. Some will be trained within a day or two, while others will need a few more days to practice.

CHAPTER 8: 48-HOURS DRAMA

24-hours

Continue to consistently apply the same instructions from Day 1, with the wisdom learned by observing your child's patterns and responses.

On day two, you can go outside for an hour in the afternoon after urinating in the bathroom.

Don't show frustration about accidents or when your child doesn't seem to understand yet. There are times when the child (who was used to disposables) is testing it. They want to see if they can get the diaper back since it was so much easier to leave. Don't give up, stay positive and happy, and they will soon realize that you are not giving up.

It possibly day 1. However, don't squeeze your youngster. Unwind and let her learn at her own pace - she's nearer to becoming accustomed to it than previously. Empower her with delicate updates and stories. Your youngster needs most to satisfy her, and commending her will mention a great job she is doing.

There may still be partial failures; it is no longer an absolute mess. On day 2, your child can learn to recognize the feeling she first felt when she needed to go to the bathroom, so she will want to be on time.

At first, a child may feel astonished to know that they already know what to do, but it can be a bit awkward and try to hide, but if you pick this up as a sign and put it in the bathroom, then give it a favorite manuscript to help her. to relax, she will defecate in comfort. "Hi, that's great! You're doing it now! Once a kid can successfully pull off, the rest can be more manageable. But we still need to be consistent and not be disappointed in following the training routine.

If a child is becoming more difficult, start yelling or resist any incentive, stay positive, and relieve the pressure.

48th hour

On the 48th hour, you can go out for an hour in the morning and an hour in the afternoon, again immediately after urinating. This helps reinforce the child that she needs to urinate before going out and gives her enough time to go inside the house and be near the bathroom before urinating again.

Wear only a loose shirt, underwear, and pants when you are out of the house. Do not wear diapers or pull-ups when you are outdoors, as either of these can signal to the brain that there is something there to "catch" the poop or pee and cause regressions.

There may be a surprise on the 48th hour, especially if you approached the 48-hour Method with no pressure of expectations. Instead of having the same thing as days 1, your child can have it suddenly and be accident-free all day!

But if a child keeps showing that she doesn't seem to have it, don't be discouraged. Your brain, body, and muscles are already receiving it. Just stay positive, reminding your child of the parts of the training she can do. It also helps to continue doing activities that you both enjoy between breaks: manuscripts, games, ice cream cones, baking cookies, etc.

A child's stamina will soften once the potty proves to be a comforting place. She can make efforts to verbalize instead of just pointing, "Mommy, potty," and she will gladly sit down on the potty. Even if nothing happens, she is still making an effort. At least she is sitting on it. It will also help if an older brother comes home from school and is cheering for her.

Of course, 48th hour could also turn into a collapse, where it seems that the progress made on days 1 is unraveling. But don't give up.

Ask your husband or another adult to watch your child for a while, then go outside to let off steam and cry. The cooling will bring new ideas on how to approach incentives in a more motivating way.

CHAPTER 9: MAKING PROGRESS

Once you have taken the steps and are getting results gradually, the following step ensures you continue getting results. Regression is a common occurrence in potty training. Even though it is unfortunate, you should know that accidents or mistakes are common and are part of the potty-training process. The good news is that it is possible to limit the frequency of these accidents.

First, you have to set reasonable expectations for your child. For example, your child no longer pees in her pants during the day doesn't mean she may not during the nighttime. You can use various methods in potty training under different conditions and environments such as daycare, public places, potty training siblings together and separately, and nighttime potty training.

When or if accidents happen, do not show frustration in front of your child. Remain positive and take measures to help your child maintain the progress. It would be best if you tried to find out the cause of the accident. They can occur for various reasons, such as health issues like diarrhea, constipation, or some other sickness, anxiety, or stress. It can also be a distraction or just a mistake.

We'll take you through how you can maintain your progress and methods to use under various circumstances.

Keep Learning

One thing you must know is that there is no "magical" method to adopt to potty train your child and maintain the results. Potty training is a continuous learning process for you and your child. It would be best if you studied your child to find out which method suits her. Even when you are getting results with a technique you are using, read about other potty-training methods, especially if you plan to have another child. What worked for the first child may not bring the same results when training the second child. Each child is unique.

Making the Results Stable for Girls

Some experts believe it is easier to maintain potty training results for girls, as they begin a little earlier and are easy to train than boys. However, making the results stable requires consistency and overall patience.

Always try your best to maintain the usual bathroom routines and habits. If any change must be introduced, do it gradually, as a sudden change can confuse your child.

Let your child have her favorite doll with her when using her potty. You can also let the child observe her big sister or Mommy use the toilet. It is advisable to use cotton underwear instead of switching to diapers, though you'll have more clean-up.

The most important thing is to maintain a positive environment. If accidents happen, do not overreact, but instead try to find the cause and look for ways to get back on track. Make sure to repeat the potty-training instructions and routine to the child and let her recite them.

Another way of making sure the results are stable is to let the child acquire some independence in using the bathroom. Teach the child how to wipe herself correctly (from front to back) and wash her hands after being done. With time, these processes will become a habit, and accidents will be very infrequent.

CHAPTER 10: POOP

One of the most common situations that parents will experience when potty training is that their child will find peeing in the potty easy, but they are more hesitant about bowel movements. If your child is a bit reluctant to poop in the potty, don't view this as a problem, but instead as a normal part of the potty-training process. Many parents will find that their child will hold themselves until a diaper or pull-up is put on them, and then they will poop in the diaper. This probably can last for years, and sometimes until the parents are frantic to get them fully potty trained for school.

First off, I understand that you may be seeing a lot of other three-year-olds being bragged about on Facebook for being successfully potty trained, and it could feel like yours is the only one that is still having problems. The truth of the matter is that the skill of peeing and pooping requires different neural pathways and other muscular systems that will often mature at different times. I assure you that a lot of children suffer from the same problem.

There is a reason why Pinterest is full of lollipop charts and M&Ms for good poops. These tricks are sometimes enough to get your child comfortable with pooping on the potty. That said, if the rewards aren't working for your kid, it is because they are afraid. Below, we will discuss four different tips to help your child find pooping in the potty easier. Before that, we will consult a couple of things you should consider before diving into these tips.

The Hurtful Poop

The majority of children who refuse to poop in the potty have a history of experiencing a poop that hurt. Before you try to deny this, remember that poop pain is a very personal experience. What you may think seems to be a typical experience could be seen as painful to somebody else.

One tricky situation is painful constipation. Even children who have a regular poop each day can end up getting constipated. You didn't read that last sentence wrong. Outside of hydration and diet, part of constipation in children is that they are great at not finishing things. This includes picking up their toys to clearing their dinner plates. Children are great at doing just the bare minimum needed to survive, and then they play. Pooping is no exception.

The busy child will only stop releasing a bit of poop for a moment, but they won't sit still long enough to evacuate their bowels fully. With time, this is going to back them up. Once poop gets backed up, it will become harder for their body to give them the right signal that they have to go. Once they receive this signal, the process can end up hurting. If they are using the potty when this happens, they will associate the pain as being the fault of the potty chair. This causes them no to want to poop on the potty.

On the off chance that your little one will not utilize the restroom; you have to ensure that they have a great deal of certainty that the crap won't hurt them. To do this, you have to ensure that they can have a "delicate serve frozen yogurt" consistency crap for a little while before you attempt to have the crap in the potty. There are a few over-the-counter items out there to do this. You can utilize PEG-or polyethylene glycol-based stool conditioners, blockage drug that contains Senna, and other such things. You can even converse with your youngster's primary care physician to perceive what they would suggest. This is something you can choose to do a long time before your 48-hours potty preparing, yet this is additionally something you may find that you need to do after your youngster has just been potty prepared because no one can tell when obstruction may occur.

Their Position

The following thing you have to look at is the position they are in when pooping. To defecate successfully, you have to move a mass of stuff through a tiny hole. This entire process requires a very complicated sequence of muscles and nerves to work together. There have been scientists who have studied pooping mechanics through radiographic imaging and observation. These studies have found that there is a particular body position that is optimal for pooping. This is called the hip flexion position. You want your knees slightly about the hips.

The ideal approach to get this hip flexion position in children and grown-ups is to furnish them with a stage stool. You need to ensure that the seat is sufficiently tall for them to rest their feet level on and brings their knees over their hips. A substitute alternative, and is a convenient solution when utilizing a public bathroom, permits your child to sit in reverse on the restroom. This will give them a more significant amount of the seat under their thighs, wiping out the impression that they will "fall in" and help them unwind.

Tip #1: Full-Fat Foods Equal Easier Poops

The body needs to have fat and fiber to poop, but you should slow down on prunes and prune juice because high-fiber foods can work in reverse if you use too much. This is why it is sometimes better to use healthy full-fat foods to keep their poops soft. One great and tasty way to do this is to make them a smoothie using full-fat coconut milk. Avocado is another good healthy fat option. Mix in their favorite fruits, and they're sure to love it.

Tip #2: Give Them Some Privacy

This might sound a bit obvious, but it is something that tends to get overlooked. When it comes to potty training, parents usually are continually watching their child see the first signs of needing to potty and then watching them potty. A lot of toddlers have already developed a sense of shame, which they have learned from us, so if you are always watching them as they use the potty, they could find it tougher to poop.

Do you find it easy if you feel like you have to poop on command? No, right? You can't poop unless you are relaxed. So, start giving them some personal space when they are pooping. Step outside of the bathroom when they are using the potty.

Tip #3: Try Praise Over Celebration

This isn't to say that praise will work against, but you should be mindful of the type of recognition you use during potty training. Praise tends to backfire during potty training. You should try to avoid turning a poop in the potty as a full-scale celebration because they type of recognition can end up stalling the progress. You may be asking, how is praising hurting your progress?

For some, the toddlers will start to feel as if there is this new pressure. They worry, "What if I can't do that again?" Potty training works better when you focus on making the process seem familiar. We all poop and pee in the potty. You wouldn't do a happy dance and call up Grandma when they brush their teeth. The same goes for pooping. It needs to be seen as just as usual as brushing your teeth.

Tip #4: Open-Door Bathroom

If you haven't already started letting your child go to the bathroom with you, this is when you should start. By having an open-door policy for your bathroom will help to make the whole process more familiar for your child. You want them to see that pooping in the potty is something everything does, even grownups.

The Process of The Poop

If those four tips don't seem to be working, I've got one more thing for you to try. You can easily breakdown the process of pooping in the potty into small steps that your child will find more achievable that can receive rewards and praise. What you need to do is use their "comfort place" to your advantage. The diaper should become your tool. And this is something you may want to think about doing before your 48-hours potty training time. It will merely get them to use to the idea of pooping on the potty.

First, keep your child bare-bottomed, or in their underwear, all day. You can permit them to ask for their diaper whenever they have to poop. When they ask for the diaper, head to the bathroom, and put the diaper on them. Then you can leave the bathroom, but they have to stay there to poop. Once they are done, clean them up and put their underwear back in the bathroom. Praise and reward them for asking in time and doing it all in the correct room. It may not seem like much, but it is a significant first step.

Depending on how your child progresses, the following step would be to have them sit on the potty when using their diaper to poop. This helps to associate the potty with something that they are comfortable with. Please continue with the cleaning process once they are done. That's the second big step.

You can do the following thing: start cutting a hole in the diaper to allow the poop to fall out. This should be done without their knowledge. Since they have been sitting on the potty when they need to poop, they will naturally poop in the potty. When they do, you can say, "See? You just pooped in the potty." Eventually, they will realize that they don't need the diaper.

Whether you do it this way or not, the point is to break down the pooping process into smaller chunks that they can easily reach.

During this process, the most important thing is to make sure that you don't punish or shame them for not feeling comfortable to poop in the potty. While you may want to get them potty trained during these 48-hours, every child is different, and you can't force them to do something they don't want to do. That can end up creating more problems than resolving them. If they need to use the potty and they don't have a diaper, and they don't feel comfortable on the potty, they are just going to hold themselves until they become constipated or have an accident.

CHAPTER 11: FIRST ATTEMPTS AT POTTY TRAINING

Sadly, potty training happens at a time when a child learns to be more confident. Your infant, known as the "terrible twos," will avoid potty workout entirely. Still, dirty your fabric, treat different toilets for different caregivers and usually cause potty activities to harm the parents. But do not despair. Even if parents are still calm and comprehensive and make potty training fun, potty training may yet be done.

First, ensure that your child is ready and set up your child's potty workout. These two steps are the basis for fast potty training without stress. Refusing to use the potty train can be frustrating; even if it is 'maintained' for long periods rather than using the potty, it can have actual health consequences. Should not hesitate to contact the pediatrician if there is a long time of resistance.

Rewarding your kid is a positive way of making your child less stubborn in the potty-training cycle. Have her or she assists in choosing awards. Visit the local toy shop, for example, and buy certain new items your child may not have until specific goals are met. You may also want to discuss with your child what she or she can do if she or she is educated in the potty (dwell at grandma's night, attend school, visit friends, etc.). The drive for good pottery training is the key.

Talk to your child if they are usually well done, but highly resistant to potty workouts. Your child might be afraid to use a potty seat. Use a potty chair on her or her and decorate the chair with stickers instead. For example, some kids are fearful of a bigger toilet flushing sound. Wait until your child leaves the room to flush, or if the toilet itself is to rinse it, even if they use it and at certain times of the day. You may also want your child to watch as your older siblings and family use the toilet to show that your child is not afraid.

It is acceptable to punish the child if it thinks she is wrong. You would decide to discipline your child if, for example, she would not let you change her dirty pair, even though you were told when you had to go. Try punishing misconduct, such as hitting the tangle or tossing the jam.

Punishment, on the other hand, is not suitable for injuries. Remember that it may just not be known that your child has to wear clothes. Even with older children, sometimes accidents happen, mainly when they are distracted by the urination during play until it is too late to go to the toilet. Try to understand that so that your child will not resist using the bathroom anymore.

Many tools are available on the market to enjoy potty training. Your child will not be as reactive if you make it a fun business, and the cycle is much quicker. Use various games, songs, and activities to teach your child how to use this pot. Remember that every child is different and will learn to use the toilet at another speed.

What Do You Do If You Do Not Do Potty Training?

Are you hitting a wall? Are you? Does not your child progress despite the numerous efforts you have made? Would you allow her to use the potty instead of her painting? Should she throw the tantrums?

Alas, you may just have chosen the wrong time to train her. Evaluate her training to ensure that she displays any signs of being potty trained emotionally.

When she doesn't want to start potty training in 48-hours, it could only be more comfortable to cool off and wait a few weeks. Before your child is ready, no matter what you do, it cannot be potty trained.

On the other hand, is your child profoundly receptive to the concepts of potty education but with trouble performing? Try to walk with her favorite toy by her movements.

- Steps 1: Put on her favorite doll some of her new underwear and let her take it down if you agree that you will use the potty doll.
- Step 2: Place the potty on the toy and make sure to enjoy the toy's win when the toy is effectively "gone potty!"
- Step 3: Tell your baby, she can also have a celebration when she can use the potty! A little party should be adequate to inspire her.

Now, I often do not allow treats, but it can be a bit of a snack often to get your child back into potty training. Some candy or little toys will motivate and encourage her. Purchase for her any photos of potty-training manuscripts or series of children's training shows.

All this is about inspiring and effective learning for your kids. Potty exercises are an incredibly stressful event for children, and you won't spoil her when trying to have some extra candy or toys.

Do not be discouraged from waiting a few weeks if you have to interrupt your child's exercise. You could do worse than waste your own time if you just move on in your training without checking the progress of your child. If you don't pay attention, you can turn your child off to the idea of potty training.

The secret to your child's easy and fast training is to wait until she is ready for this cycle physically and emotionally. If you have had a stressful event such as a relocation, daycare, or a little brother or sister brought into your life, you may not be ready to make another significant change right now. Nothing is wrong, waiting for your child to become more open to change.

CHAPTER 12: POTTY TRAINING AND CAREGIVERS

One way to confuse your child and make the potty-training process take even longer is by not having everyone who takes care of your child on the same page. If you have gotten this far in the manuscript, you are most likely choosing this method to use when potty training your child. Any person who is with your child in the bathroom should become knowledgeable about this plan. I have seen more than one argument between parents when reading the list and the other parent has not. Don't let that be you.

Partner Up

Communicate with your partner. If you have been the one potty training your child at home, then you will know your child's cues and have a whole method down with her in the bathroom. Your partner may not have had as many opportunities to be involved with the process. Be patient. If your partner is keeping an eye on the child while you shower or run errands, explain the specific things to look for when your child might have to go to the bathroom, and some things to avoid, such as letting her watch TV or play on the iPad.

At School

Your child's teacher will be willing to help as much as possible and should be a significant part of your support system, but unless the school has a potty-training program, it is not the teacher's job to potty train your child. Let the teacher know the best way to support your child during the school day, but if there are too many accidents at school, the teacher will, most likely, tell you your child needs to go back to wearing diapers when not at home—which will just confuse and hinder your kiddo during training. It will take time for your child to get used to going to the bathroom in a different place, with a different person, and with other procedures, so let your child's teacher know what kinds of things to do or say to help your child keep her underwear dry.

Talk with your child about going to the bathroom at school before you send her back. For example, "Little Bob, you have done such a good job going pee and poop on the potty at home; now you will use the potty at school, too. At home, you tell Mommy when you need to go potty, and at school, you will tell your teacher." Before you leave the child for the day, it helps to have a conversation among the three of you, so your child knows both of you support her in the same way.

One good rule of thumb is to bring your child to the bathroom she will use at school as soon as you drop her off. Doing this gives her the chance to go to the bathroom with you, the person she's most comfortable with, which will make her feel more comfortable using the school's bathroom. Not only that but knowing she has emptied her bladder at the beginning of the school day means she should be able to stay dry for a couple of hours, which helps the teacher know when to start giving your child extra bathroom reminders. You should also get into the habit of having her go right before leaving school, as well; that way, you have the car ride covered, too.

everywhere else

It's always a good habit to bring a newly potty-trained kid to the bathroom immediately upon arriving at any new location. Nothing is worse than getting halfway through with grocery shopping, only to have your child tell you she needs to go to the bathroom.

Five Tips for Caregivers Who Aren't You

If you can't get your partner or other caregivers to read this plan, these are the five most important things they should know.

1. Try not to inquire whether she needs/needs to go to the washroom: "Reveal to me when you have to go."
2. Try not to disregard the kid in a room.
3. Be available for every mishap so you can divert the kid in her misfortune rather than after the accident.
4. Give rewards and applause for each time she effectively goes potty.
5. Try not to show outrage or dissatisfaction.

CHAPTER 13: YOUR CHILD'S BEHAVIOR AND POTTY TRAINING

The standard line offered to the parent of a child who's hard to train is, "No child has gotten on the school bus in a nappy yet." This, of course, is not much help if you are trying to picture out how to proceed.

If your child has progressed from the terrible twos to the formidable fours without showing the toilet's slightest interest, your concern is justified. If your child prefers to squat, comfortably nappies, in a dark corner, holding a special blanket, you may be dealing with physical or emotional complications, irrational fears, or ingrained habit. You may have a willful child who needs special handling or dealing with a simple semantics problem.

It's also possible that your timing is off. Asynchrony is a big word that means that a child's "internal clock" is set differently from other family members. Elimination may not occur when you think it should. For example, a child may have only one bowel movement in two days. If this is the case, it's you who will have to do the adjusting.

And, painful but real, you may be causing the trouble. Ask yourself the questions listed in the box below. If you have two or three "yes" answers, perhaps you should sit back and do a little thinking. Try talking out your spouse's problems, a friend, a doctor, or nurse practitioner-but don't take your frustrations out on your child.

Some Questions to Ask Yourself

- Are you determined to have your child toilet trained by a certain age or stage in her or her life, or at some particular point in your own?

- Do you see your life as being in a shamble until your child is trained?

- Are you unusually sensitive to pressure from family or friends to "get that child to use the toilet"?
- Do you think your child is punishing you by not cooperating with your training efforts?
- Are you optimistic that because your child can understand you, there's no reason toilet training can't be accomplished easily?
- Have you ever been described as a "controlling" parent?
- Are you vehemently opposed to backing off for now and trying again in a month when all the pieces might fall into place?

One possible solution might be to have someone else take over. Sometimes, for all our good intentions, we are too emotionally involved to get the job done. Some parents can't teach their teenagers to drive, and wisely turn the task over to someone who's better able to deal with it unemotionally. This doesn't mean they're bad parents. They're to be congratulated for recognizing the problem and taking the proper steps to correct it. It's the same with toilet training. If you can see that the process is getting you too upset and that you, in turn, are upsetting your child, try to find someone else with some emotional distance who can do it for you. And don't feel guilty! Part of being a good parent is knowing what you can and can't do. You won't prove anything by trying to do the impossible.

Physical Complications

If you suspect that it's a physical problem, have your child checked thoroughly by a physician.

- Consider the chance of sensitivity. Lactose narrow mindedness (the powerlessness to process milk or milk items) is the most well-known, yet different nourishments can cause hypersensitivities.
- How much sorbitol is your kid expending in sugarless confections and gum? Sorbitol is another guilty party in incessant

free stools. It is likewise found commonly in pear juice and squeezed apple, having any effect if a kid drinks parcels.

- Observe for signs of urinary infections. These involve pain or burning sensations while urinating, straining to urinate, color variations in the urine, foul-smelling urine, repeated urination that generates very little, or a tearing watercourse of urine.

More marks might be abdominal pain or a fever of a shaky foundation. Such illnesses are not exceptional in small children.

- Be mindful that even after a urinary issue has cleared up, the youngster may, in any case, recall and dread the agony of peeing, and this may confound potty preparing. Console the kid, and don't be anxious if it takes the person in question some time to get over the dread.

My daughter, at age four, would often have accidents-to my distress. I thought she was being lazy and refusing to stop her play to take the time to go to the bathroom, which she knew how to do. I was on her case a lot. At our annual physical, we discovered it was a physical problem. My guilt load was sober for a long time. - Martha Berk

- Investigation, a toilet-trained child who starts to have many urinary accidents and a significant increase in diabetes urination.
- Remember that the runs tireless runny, free stools can cause issues with entrail control. Tenacious loose bowels usually are an indication of a physical problem, and a specialist should treat it.
- Consider the likelihood that clogging is shielding your youngster from needing to move their entrails since it is difficult. If it's not ceaseless, you can help by staying with the youngsters. At the same time, they're perched on the restroom, greasing up the rear-end with Vaseline, or in any event, helping hold the "cheeks" separated to make it simpler to move the insides. Dietary changes can likewise help. Ceaseless stoppage can squeeze the bladder

and cause daytime just as evening, mishaps in which case its chance to look for clinical consideration.

Emotional Complications

Don't dally seek professional help if you think there's an emotional problem you can't solve. Getting help from a therapist doesn't mean that your child is in serious trouble, and you may find that things improve rapidly after only a session or two. Children are often more open with a neutral third-party person than with a parent. Remember that children usually keep silent about fear or shame they're feeling. Therapists are trained to help children learn to express and deal with these feelings.

- Remember that the emotional makeup of a human being is too complicated. It's not realistic to expect that just because a child is small in stature, they will have a short-range of emotions. And handling all these strange feelings and sensations is doubly hard for a child because of her or her undeveloped wisdom and lack of information.

- Watch for interference from others. Siblings can set a child off by playing on fears and expectations; friends or even teachers may say the wrong thing.

- Ask your child to show you how they would toilet train a doll or stuffed animal. Watch the child's behavior and listen carefully to commands and instructions. If the child uses abusive language, scolds, and handles the toy roughly, it might be a clue that your own or someone else's attitudes and actions are at fault.

- Or get the child to draw a picture of a bathroom. Ask for explanations of anything you don't understand. You may get some clues about worries or fears the child has been repressing.

Toilet Fears

Some children, especially those with older storytelling siblings, believe a toilet is a hiding place for sharks, alligators, or water monsters. The sound of a toilet flushing may serve to confirm this. On discovering that her child feared the monsters in the toilet, one mother led her child to the bathroom, called the monsters up out of the bathroom, and blew them out the window, much to the child's relief.

Don't flush the toilet while the child is still sitting on it. Many children find the noise and action frightening and worry about being "swallowed up." Showing a child how things work inside the toilet tank and taking the child to the basement to explain the workings' plumbing system may banish this fear.

Willfulness

If you have a genuinely willful child, you will have seen stubbornness and other signs before now. They don't usually begin to appear just at this time. If you have seen the signs before, look back and remember how you've handled your stubborn child who sometimes digs in their heels and refuses to cooperate.

Sometimes a three- or four-year-old child stubbornly refuses to make a bowel movement in the toilet or potty and insists on nappies even when the child uses the potty or toilet appropriately when urinating. Sometimes a child even insists on taking underwear off and putting a nappy on just before a BM. It's frustrating because it's obvious the child feels the coming BM's sensation and can exercise control to go when they want to. Besides, children who retain BMs for any significant length of time are more likely to become constipated. Sitting a child on the toilet for long periods is unnecessary when a child understands how to use it. Children who have been lectured or reminded too often, and forced to sit on the toilet for long periods against their will, may understandably be resistant to your pressure when control is the issue.

There is no single explanation for this situation. For a child who might be stuck in this behavior and for whom even rewards don't work, and you don't think constipation is the problem, change your approach. Back off for a few weeks. Wait for a stress-free week, and then tell your child that you're not having any more nappies when this box of nappies is gone. Transfer all responsibility to your child, explaining that "It's your job to make your BM and get it into the toilet. You no longer need my help." Explain that it's okay if your child has a BM or wets, but they can't walk around in soiled underwear. Clean clothes must be worn before engaging in any other activity.

You Can Also:

- Consider using reverse psychology: "Oh, I'm sure you won't want to use the potty today: we'll just put the nappy on." Or switch roles: "I need to go potty. Will you keep me company?"
- Avoid "no" answers as much as possible by telling your child, "It's time to try" instead of asking, "Do you have to go?"
- Give choices: "Do you want to help get your pants off and wipe yourself, or should I do it?" "Do you want to use the potty chair today or the big toilet? /J
- Physically lead the child to the toilet with a hand on a shoulder or arm, not roughly, but firmly enough, so the child knows you mean business.
- Increase un-constipating foods at mealtime. Keep a matter-of-fact attitude in the face of tantrums and accidents, and show no annoyance.
- Think of your child just as a "late bloomer" to help you avoid feeling frustrated.

- Discuss this with your child's day-care provider as it may provide additional insights and offer you both new ways to handle this problem.
- Completely back off. Possibly your style and your child's temperament are working against each other.

CHAPTER 14: ELIMINATION COMMUNICATION

Elimination Communication (EC) can instigate as early as birth or as late as parents are comfortable. Still, parents typically begin using EC between birth and four months. This is a clean, all-natural way to teach your child from the beginning how to recognize and control her bodily functions.

What Is Elimination Communication?

Elimination Communication, also identified as Infant Potty Training or Natural Infant Hygiene, focuses on caregivers recognizing an infant's signals and having her pee or poop in a toilet bowl or waste container rather than in a diaper. Using sounds and movements to communicate between the parent and infant works to strengthen the bond, increases communication, and ultimately makes for a smoother transition into final potty training. Although your child will not be eliminating waste independently until she is fully mobile, she will be more likely to potty train faster and use bathroom facilities alone at an earlier age if you begin with EC.

How Does EC Work?

Elimination Communication links to a timeless practice, still widespread in Europe and Asia, where parents and caregivers learn to watch and listen to infants when it comes time to pee or poop. By focusing more directly on your baby's bathroom needs in much the same way you focus on your baby's nutrition needs, you can enable yourself to avoid common, everyday parenting issues such as fussy babies, dirty diapers, leaky diapers, and more. EC follows several simple steps to help parents and infants adapt naturally to what has always been a natural progression toward potty training.

Step 1: Know Your Baby

Many parents see this step, and they feel inclined to move on right away. Of course, you know your baby! It is your baby, after all. However, EC requires you to understand your baby on a more intimate level than diapered babies. For EC to work, you need to know your baby's routine in eating and sleeping and peeing and pooping. How often is she going to the bathroom? How long does she wait after eating before she eliminates waste from her system? How often does she pee or poop while sleeping? The solutions to all of these queries will help you to know ahead of time when to watch for your baby's bathroom signals.

Essential

Many mothers wonder why they have not heard of Elimination Communication before. While EC is a commonly used practice in some cultures, it is still not necessarily a recommended practice for modern-day families in the United States. Pediatricians vary on whether or not they endorse this practice, so there is no one easy answer to whether or not Elimination Communication is better or worse than traditional potty training.

You also need to get to know your baby's signals. Many parents report babies kicking their legs, kicking off blankets, waking from a deep sleep, flaring their nostrils, refusing to latch on when nursing, squirming, passing gas, unexplained crying, and intense looks of concentration as signs their children are preparing to eliminate. These signs are common in infants, but you must watch for your own child's signals. There is no one universal signal that will indicate when an infant is preparing to eliminate. As you focus more on your child's movements and needs, you will become more aware of which unique signals work for her.

Alert

Not all mothers will pick up on their children's signals right away. It takes time and practice to learn when your baby is signaling and what each movement means. Don't get discouraged if it takes you weeks or even months to know how your baby communicates. At the same time, you should be prepared for your baby's signals to change as she develops and matures.

Step 2: Use an Elimination Container

Once you have become aware of your child's signals, it is time to begin using a toilet or basin. As soon as you notice your child signaling that she will eliminate, remove any pants, diapers, or blankets that may be in the way. Then, hold your child over the elimination container so she can proceed.

The way you hold your child is incredibly important. Parents often feel inclined to keep their children at arms' length with the child's legs dangling. In other words, parents usually want the maximum distance possible between the waste and themselves. While it may be ideal for you to minimize your contact with your child's pee or poop, such a hold will more than likely frighten your child, making her either too nervous about eliminating or else so worried that she stops out of fear rather than out of a natural need. When and where to pee or poop is lost on a child held in this fashion.

Instead, you should look for a hold that provides security for the baby and comfort for you. You should find a way to hold your child that keeps her feeling safe and protected as she learns this new lesson about peeing and pooping. Try cradling her behind her shoulders and under her knees. If that doesn't work, consider waiting until she has enough muscle control to allow you to hold her under her arms, making sure to support her head and allowing her to assume a sitting position on your basin. As you and your infant progress with EC, you will instinctively find the hold that works best for you.

Your baby won't learn right away when it is time to pee or poop, so you want to make sure you are prepared to hold her in a particular place for several minutes. Many parents have reported success using the same potty chairs that other parents use for potty-training toddlers. In contrast, other parents move right to the toilet. Still, other parents select a smaller plastic basin or bowl that they designate as the "elimination container." Whichever container you choose is up to you, but it is essential to see how specific sizes and materials may benefit your baby.

Remember that there is no "standard" elimination container; find one that works best for you and your baby, experimenting with several different ones. Smaller containers allow you to hold your child in such a way that she grows accustomed to wrapping her legs on the sides of the box in much the same way she will when she uses a regular toilet. Mobile potty chairs or plastic containers are more accessible for you as parents. However, they are messier to clean and care for than a typical bathroom. Porcelain toilet bowls tend to be colder, which will increase the discomfort level for some infants as you begin elimination communication.

Fact

As you choose your elimination container, you need to remember that one of the goals of EC is proper hygiene. In addition to finding a box that is safe and comfortable for you and your baby, you also need to be prepared to clean and sanitize this container after each use. Most basic dishwashing and house cleaning products will work to clean and sanitize your container.

Step 3: Communicate with Your Child

As you work on EC with your child, you will listen for sounds from her indicating she is ready to go to the bathroom. Simultaneously, you can also use sounds to show her you are prepared for her to begin eliminating. These sounds not only work to help the EC process but also encourage your child to use sounds as a means to communicate with you as the parent at an earlier age, without necessarily resorting to crying.

Once you have begun to hold your child over the basin, start making a soft sound in her ear. Many parents report success with sounds that imitate the sound of water flow, such as "sssssss" or "pepepepe." The idea here is that your child will begin to associate this sound with the time to release her bladder and move her bowels. In the beginning, this will work to help her know when you are ready. You can begin scheduling times for her to go to the bathroom much the same way you might ask your older child to use the bathroom before you leave the house. You are communicating to your infant you are ready for her to eliminate (even if she is not). As your child progresses, you will soon notice her using these sounds to communicate back to you when she needs to go to the bathroom. This is another sign that you have strengthened your bond with your child and increased her level of communication. Working with her on one of her most basic needs benefits both you and your child on multiple fronts.

Step 4: Maintain A Relaxed, Flexible, And Positive Attitude

EC is just like potty training in that it can be frustrating for the parent and the infant. However, you must stay calm and uplifting throughout the process. Messes are a natural part of an infant's life—regardless of whether you use EC or not—so don't get upset. Your infant will sense your discomfort or frustration, and you will see a corresponding response from her. For these reasons, it is essential to remember that accidents will happen. Your baby will need you to be flexible about when she eliminates, how she eliminates, and how quickly she picks up on the methods you've chosen. She will also need you to maintain a positive attitude about her progress. EC experts typically discourage parents from using either punishments or rewards when training your child. However, it is still essential to maintain an attitude that will work for both you and your infant. Remember, she will take her cues from you on mentality just as much as they will about be feeding, eliminating, and more. You are her leader in every way, and, after all, she is brand new here!

Obstacles To EC

Elimination Communication is not right for everyone. Parents who choose to use EC are most often people who practice Attachment Parenting or Continuum Concept Parenting. Attachment Parenting typically involves keeping the baby on the parent's body with a sling or similar hold, extending nursing schedules, and co-sleeping. This does not mean that a parent using EC must also follow all parts of the Attachment Parenting regimen. Still, many aspects of EC fit in better with a parent who is regularly and consistently with her or her child.

It is also essential to ponder who else will be taking care of your child. Daycares cannot and will not participate in EC because it is against the law and licensing codes for daycare to have a consistently un-diapered baby on the premises. Likewise, EC requires one person to be alert to the baby's signals at all times, which is generally too difficult in a situation where one person is responsible for multiple infants in the same age range. This is not to say that a parent of multiple children cannot practice EC, but multiple infants may find this too complicated. EC becomes more comfortable if some of the children are older, and thus more independent and capable of taking care of their own elimination needs.

CHAPTER 15: THE RESET

Now that you have decided which tools you are going to invest in, you will also want to take some time to observe your child's behavior in preparation for creating your basic potty routine. There's no need to set alarms or stick to rigid schedules in the beginning. Over-prompting can backfire and cause your little one to reverse course quickly.

You will want to take note over about a week when your child usually dirties a diaper and then prompt your child to go to the potty before those times. Initially, you will want to encourage your child to go at critical times of the day, plus the times you note. The essential times are usually around transition times like waking up, after meals, before leaving the house, arriving home, and before bed. Generally, your child should have the opportunity to go roughly once every 30–60 minutes in the beginning to increase the number of successes she will have. After a limited day, you may notice a pattern on what times your child is using the potty most. Use these times as your new prompt times and continue to go if your child states an additional need. You will see the number of trips to the bathroom naturally decrease. Soon enough, your child will recognize the urge to go and will start informing you reliably when the need arises. This will virtually eliminate the need to watch the clock overall. However, you will still want to use your transition points (after meals, as soon as you get home from a shopping trip, etc.) as a reminder to at least try to sit on the potty.

In the beginning, you will also desire to keep your child very well hydrated. Load up on morning liquids and then gradually decrease as the day goes on. Your child will learn faster if there are more opportunities for success. You want to purposefully cue that feeling quite often as you start training your toddler. Conversely, you don't want to have a big accident while your child sleeps. This is why you should taper off liquids within the day. Try not to give your child any fluids within an hour of bedtime.

Be consistent in your approach to potty training. Your child is relying on you to help them be successful. If you chance to be out at the store and your little one indicates that it's time to go to the potty, it is best to drop everything and go. In time, you will get a little bit more time to get to the bathroom, but in the beginning, you may have very little time at all. This is one cause why many people choose to spend the first few days or even the first week at home. There is nothing wrong with staying close to home initially, but using a public restroom is part of the training and development that needs to occur. While you can do it after, it may be preferable to introduce this event earlier, mainly because it requires your child to repeat the success at home into other locations. Some children have a tough time announcing the need to go potty in public. Still, you need to help your child overcome that hurdle because accidents in public are far more embarrassing and can cause your child to regress wanting to wear a diaper.

Your routine should also focus specifically on your little one's daytime potty habits. While some methods might advocate for putting daytime and nighttime training together, this is usually only successful with older children (36+ months), mostly due to physical development. For this reason, you will crave to continue to use diapers or pull-ups overnight. If you notice, however, that your child is waking dry on her or her own, after a full night's sleep, you may want to talk about night-time potty routines.

Part of your child's routine also needs to include fostering independence throughout the potty process. Ideally, you desire your child to be completely self-sufficient while washing and drying hands or pulling pants on or off. In the beginning, though, your child will look to you for help. Using a visual chart for a reminder of what to do is one sure way to help your child get in and out of the bathroom more independently. This is important because, eventually, when it's time for your child to use the potty at night, you won't want to have to wake up to take them to help with one step of the process, like drying her or her hands or pulling up pants.

Likewise, you want to minimize your time interacting in the potty process, but if your child needs help, prompt them to ask for it. This will allow you to stay a little bit more removed from the actual activity and not end up with your child just relying on you to take care of their need. For example, if your child has gone in the potty and is having trouble wiping afterward but hasn't asked you for help, you might say something like, "Good job going potty! Do you need help wiping?"

Sometimes, a child gets frustrated and just stops trying or starts to cry. This is an excellent time to ask, "Can you ask for help simply?" This way, your toddler begins to understand that you aren't going to take over when things get tough. In certain times of a day, you may find a different need for help, especially when your child is tired.

Just Before You Begin

Once you have made your purchases and decisions about all these necessary items to help your little one has an easier time learning to use the potty, it's time to put all your gear in place. For a limited day leading up to starting to potty train, you'll want to spend time throughout the day talking about how fun it is to go potty and get rid of messy diapers. You will want to retake a tour of the bathroom, go over the picture chart, read potty manuscripts, sing songs, and make it sound like the immense fun your child will have all year! Confirm you are modeling the behaviors you want your toddler to learn and invite them to sit on the potty afterward to you when you have to go, help you flush, and even wash hands for practice.

You will also want to have a quick chat with any child care providers because they will have to be included in this process. Let your provider know your expectations and the words you would like to use to communicate potty needs and ask them how you can accommodate them, such as providing a chart for them to help you keep track of your child's progress.

CHAPTER 16: SPECIAL CIRCUMSTANCES

Has your child overcome many potty-training hurdles but continues to wet the bed at night? Have chronic wetting or soiling accidents? Have problems with constipation or urination? If you reflect, your child might have a medical problem, turn to your child's pediatrician for help.

Getting Help

If you're having problems with potty training, the first person to turn to for help is your child's pediatrician. Doctors with this specialty work with potty training problems day in and day out and are incredibly knowledgeable about the subject. In addition to their technical knowledge, pediatricians have dealt with hundreds or even thousands of youngsters, which gives them a substantial basis for comparison. Although it may be true that no one knows your child as well as you do, professionals are in a better position to be objective about your child's capabilities.

When talking to your child's doctor, be honest and forthcoming when sharing your potty-training problems, as well as the steps you have taken to correct them — even if it means admitting things that you have said and done that you think were wrong. To hold back is to do your child and yourself a disservice. The truth is that no parent feels very confident about how they have handled all of the difficult problems that can arise during potty training, and if they do, they probably shouldn't!

If you don't feel comfortable confiding in your child's pediatrician, schedule some interviews, and find a different doctor. Since there's nothing like hearing other parents' struggles to give you a new perspective on your own, consider joining a parenting group, too.

Staying Dry at Night

If children have bladder control during the day, they are likely to have it at night, too, which means that it's time to stop using diapers. Sleepy children cannot use the potty easily if they are in diapers, so wearing diapers to bed encourages wetting and soiling. Instead, use a rubber pad to protect the ground and put waterproof pants over pull-ups so your child can get them off to use the potty at night. Or, try putting a PODS in her regular underwear.

Although full-blown fears of the dark do not typically develop until after age three, precocious children may feel uneasy at night at younger generations. Move the potty chair into the bedroom or light the way to the bathroom with nightlights. The prospect of a company can be an incentive for a little one to get out of bed at night, so encourage your child to awaken you so you can take her to the potty.

Do not let her drink many liquids after dinner, and take her to the potty before bed. Take her before you go to bed, too, and set the alarm to awaken yourself so you can take her to the bathroom once or twice a night. That may help her develop the habit of waking up to use the potty once she is mature enough to wake herself.

Essential

To avoid urinary accidents, be sure your child avoids caffeine like the plague. Read the labels on coffees, teas, and sodas carefully. Avoid no caffeinated, carbonated beverages, too.

In the meantime, be patient. Most children have been conditioned to urinate in bed for several years. Disposable diapers reduce the discomfort of wetting to the point that many youngsters don't awaken even after they have had an accident, or they don't awaken because they simply sleep too deeply.

The Bedwetting Blues

There are three leading causes of bedwetting: motivational, physical, and "deep sleep." It can be hard to tell whether bedwetting stems from the I-don't-feel-like-getting-out-of-bed-to-use-the-potty-at-night syndrome parents tend to think at first.

Physical Causes

Physical problems ranging from small bladder size to a bladder infection can cause incontinence. Many can be easily corrected. Sleep apnea can prevent children from awakening to use the potty; the brain never receives the bladder's signal that it is full. Eventually, the sphincter gives way, causing an accident. If apnea is due to problems with the adenoids and tonsils, it can be easily treated. Apnea is sometimes challenging to diagnose because obvious symptoms may only be present at night, so children can appear healthy when examined by a doctor. Bedwetting also can infrequently be the result of bladder infection, a hormone deficiency, petit mal seizures, diabetes, a small bladder, a physical abnormality or malformation, or a central nervous system disorder.

Deep Sleep

Physical problems are thought to affect less than three percent of children. The usual problem which causes millions of youngsters to wet the bed is that they sleep so deeply, they simply don't awaken so they can use the potty. They may have some dry nights, but if they can't manage to go a full month without wetting the bed, the diagnosis may turn out to be "primary enuresis." What keeps them from awakening isn't understood.

Bedwetting Cures

Beware of the pediatrician who suggests your child just "isn't trying" without first doing a full medical exam (to rule out organic problems), a psychological exam (to rule out changes in the child's life that could cause increased exhaustion or stress), and a thorough family history (to investigate the possibility of an inherited problem). Since secondary enuresis is caused by stress and depression, and since punishing children causes them to feel stressed and become depressed, you must react to bedwetting gently and with kindness. Otherwise, you'll make the situation worse rather than better.

Try-for-Dry

If your child wets the bed because of a chronic inability to awaken, be careful of the many outrageously overpriced treatment programs from companies with questionable reputations that prey on desperate parents.

Restricting Fluids

The common practice of restricting fluids in the evening is a controversial cure, which probably won't help. Do eliminate liquids that irritate the bladder and increase the frequency of urination (such as caffeine), check for food allergies, and avoid lots of fluids late in the evening, but know that regular fluid intake does not cause bedwetting. Adequate hydration is necessary for your child's health. When children are dehydrated, their urine is more concentrated, which increases urinary urgency. It's the inability to awaken that drives enuresis.

Determine Patterns

If the problem is your child's inability to awaken so she can use the potty, treatments aren't much help before age five or six. Some parents claim to have reset brain wave patterns during sleep by managing to bring their children to a state of complete wakefulness several times each night when they were very young.

Bedwetting specialists recommend that parents of toddlers try to determine the time at which the accidents typically occur by conducting frequent diaper checks or outfitting children with a moisture-sensitive unit that activates an alarm when urination begins. When the unit's electrical pad is moistened, a circuit closes and rings a bell or sounds a buzzer. These were very pricey items; now, they are readily available through outlets that specialize in potty training products.

Alert!

Don't try to cure your child's bedwetting by severely cutting back on fluids. Doing so makes the urine more concentrated, so your child's urge to urinate will be more intense. When she does have to go potty, she'll have a hard time getting there fast enough.

Keep track of wetting incidents for a week. Once you've established your child's patterns, awaken her ten to twenty minutes before she is likely to wet the bed and take her to the bathroom to see if she can use it. Even if she never fully awakens, you may be able to avoid some accidents. Moreover, if you can consistently head them off for several months, you may cure the problem by conditioning her. Exactly how these conditioning works is not understood. Rather than learning to get up at night, most children who have been successfully prepared simply sleep through the night and stay dry without ever using the potty. If wetting starts up again after being conditioned, parents may need to take them to the potty every night for a few days to provide their brains with a "tune-up."

Medications

Some medications can help bedwetters, though they are not typically used with children younger than five or six.

- Imipramine (also known as Tofranil) is the most commonly prescribed medication for bedwetting. Although this tricyclic antidepressant can help older children, the many challenging side effects make its advisability questionable. They include mood changes, nightmares, constipation, dry mouth, cardiac arrhythmia, drowsiness, restless legs syndrome, hypotension, confusion, tremor, dizziness, jaw cramps, and more!

- Oxybutynin chloride is a bladder antispasmodic which has proved helpful to many bedwetters. However, Stanford University researchers Barbara R. Sommer, William Kennedy, and Ruth O'Hara, Ph.D., note that adults who use this medication begin to show impaired memory and intellectual functioning. While the effects on children have not been studied and remain unknown, these doctors believe it is likely to have the same troubling effects. Known side effects include irritability, facial flushing, irritability, and heat exhaustion during hot months.

- DDAVP or Desmopressin is the synthetic version of a hormone the body produces typically at night. It recycles water from urine and moves it back into the bloodstream, thereby decreasing the volume. That's why even though most people urinate every few hours during the day, they can sleep through the night without having to get up to use the bathroom. Although DDAVP is a standard treatment for chronic bedwetting, it has difficult side effects, including nosebleeds, flushing, hypertension, and hypotension. Besides, it can interact with a wide range of medications. Bedwetting typically resumes as soon as the drug is discontinued. Still, it is a boon to older children, who may be able to use it as needed to attend sleepovers and summer camp.

CHAPTER 17: WRAP-UP

Mastering naptime, nighttime, and poop can prove to be some of the most challenging aspects of potty training.

Naptime

There are two main aspects to potty training during sleep. Number one is developing a brain-to-bladder connection, and number two is increasing muscle control. But the simple fact is most kids are ready for naptime (and nighttime) training well before their parents realize. Often, children will be dry during sleep and pee in their diapers as soon as they wake up, giving a false impression that they've been peeing while asleep.

The five-step natural progression to staying dry during sleep is as follows:

1. Peeing without being disrupted from sleep.
2. Peeing during sleep but waking up immediately afterward from the accident.
3. Starting to pee while asleep and waking up in the middle of the accident.
4. Waking up before needing to pee.
5. Sleeping all the way through without needing to pee.

Keeping these steps in mind, you can begin to look for progress. So even if your child isn't staying dry the entire time that they're asleep, you can find some level of accomplishment and know that things are moving in the right direction. If you're lucky, your child may skip some or all of these steps and go straight to dry before potty training even starts.

Common Problems

Potty Training for Naptime Can Pose Various Challenges.

- A lack of consistency in the environment. For example, your child may nap some days at preschool, once a week at a grandparent's house, and on weekends at home. This can make it harder to maintain a consistent process. Keep all caregivers on the same page as much as possible to avoid confusion for your child.

- Daycare requirements. Even if your child is already in underwear, most daycares automatically put children who aren't considered fully potty trained in a disposable trainer for naps. To maintain consistency, you want to be sure to communicate to your child's caregivers what your wishes are for naptime. If they require a disposable trainer for napping until your child shows they can be dry consistently, you may want to consider using a cloth diaper and a waterproof mattress cover for their cot instead.

- Not limiting fluids. By not limiting your child is drinking before naptime, there is a greater chance of needing to pee while sleeping. But that's okay. Your child should get in more liquids earlier in the day so you can limit them closer to bedtime for more dry nights. It's more likely they'll hold their bladder for a two-hour nap than 10 hours overnight anyway.

- Still sleeping in a crib. If your child still naps in a crib, they won't be able to get out of bed on their own if they have the urge to use the potty. Make sure you have a baby monitor in your child's room so they can call for you if they need to go.

- The dreaded car naps. If your child still isn't staying dry during naps, the last thing you want is them falling asleep in their car seat unprotected. But instead of using a disposable trainer, keep a waterproof car seat protector in your vehicle or potty-training survival kit. Don't hesitate to use it to prevent a mess if there's any possibility your little one could fall asleep.

Best Strategies

For the fastest, most effective results, I recommend ditching naptime diapers at the same time as you initiate potty training. Not only does this keep things as consistent as possible for your child, but it also prevents them from potentially just withholding until they get their naptime disposable trainer on. Again, you are staying true to your word that there are no more diapers. Here are some of my best strategies to tackle potty training during naptime.

First and primary, you want to be sure your child's mattress is protected in case of an accident. It can be challenging to get urine stains and odor out of beds, and no one has time to deal with that. Then, on the days you're at home together, allow your child to nap bottomless for at least the first five naps. Even though your child is asleep, going bottomless still will enable them to be more aware of their body's sensations and any accidents. Encourage your child to sit on the potty to pee and poop before lying down for their nap. You can incorporate this as part of their routine so they will come to expect it. Also, wake them up about 10 minutes before they usually would wake and have them sit on the potty at that time to prevent wetting the bed. If your child stays dry for their entire nap, be sure to offer a reward and lots of praise. You want them to feel proud and empowered.

Also, provide any specific information or instructions regarding naptime potty training to your child's caregivers, so they are following the same process, setting your child up for success outside the home environment, as well.

Rest assured that as your child's daytime control improves, and their potty frequency gradually decreases, they'll start having dry naps, too.

Night Time

The topic of nighttime potty training has proven to be somewhat controversial. Many people believe that being able to stay dry throughout the night is purely a result of hormonal development. There is indeed a hormone called anti-diuretic hormone, or ADH, which we all produce as we get older, and it causes our bodies to make less urine overnight. This develops at different ages for everyone, and this aspect cannot be taught or trained. But relying on this hormonal development alone has some risks. It can end up leaving you dependent on nighttime diapers for way longer than you intended (until your child is seven years of age or older), it can prolong daytime accidents, and by not training them to be dry overnight, the muscles your child uses to control their bladder may not fully strengthen. Although we can't teach our child how to not pee during the night, we can teach them how to wake up and get to the potty if they do need to pee. And voila. Dry nights.

For your child to wake up from a deep sleep in the night to go to the potty, their brain needs to receive a signal from their bladder that it's full. With lots of persistence and practice, you can help your kid learn to recognize this signal. Eventually, your child will be able to go the entire night without needing to pee at all. As you start seeing more significant strides with their daytime potty-training progress, you'll also begin noticing overnight improvement. The earlier in the potty-training process you decide to tackle nighttime training, the better. It may feel daunting initially, but I'm going to give you the tools you need, so you have the confidence to get the job done.

Common Problems

As you can probably imagine, achieving dry nights can come with some challenges. They might include:

- Lack of sleep. You're probably worried about the lack of sleep that may come along with nighttime potty training. I won't lie to you—you might feel like you have a newborn again initially, but I promise it's very temporary and very worth it.

- Mountains of laundry. I would recommend having multiple sheets and mattress pads on hand to avoid having to do laundry every single day. To keep middle-of-the-night bed clothes changes quick and easy, layer waterproof mattress pads and sheets so when the top layer gets wet, you can peel it away and have a clean, dry layer underneath. There are even some layered disposable sheets on the market that can just be thrown out if they get soiled.

- Your child is a profound sleeper. It can make things more challenging if your child is such a deep sleeper that they don't wake up from being wet. If your child is at least three years old, you can try a bedwetting alarm, which will wake your child at the first signs of wetness and thereby help create a brain-to-bladder connection.

Best Strategies

Overall, training for daytime and nighttime simultaneously is the best and most efficient way to see results. You could potentially do both together instead of having to take the time to go back and do nighttime training separately after you have a good handle on daytime training. Alternatively, if you're already balancing your child being in underwear at home and training pants at daycare anyway, you could opt for a more gradual approach and wait until your child is self-initiating and staying dry for more extended periods throughout the day before starting nighttime potty training. Evaluate the pros and cons as they connect to your family to decide on the best time to start.

This can potentially save you some trouble (and sleep) in the long run. Here's how it works: About 15 minutes before your child usually wakes up in the morning, quietly go in and feel how wet their diaper is. This will tell you if they're peeing during the night, or if they're waiting until they first wake up in the morning to release, which is very common. Make a note of the results because you can use this information after

As you did with naptime, you want your child to stay bottomless for at least the first five nights, just like during daytime training, this aids in body awareness and the realization that there's no longer something there to catch the mess. In sleep, it will be difficult for your child to distinguish between underwear and a diaper.

It's also helpful to limit fluids after dinnertime. If your child usually takes milk or water to fall asleep, I'm not suggesting you take that away completely. Instead, cut the amount they typically get in half, so it's no more than four ounces. The comfort they get is more about the habit of drinking than about the quantity. It would be safest if you encouraged your child to drink most of their fluids earlier in the day, so they remain hydrated.

This means have your child pee once at the beginning of their bedtime routine and then again right before they climb into bed.

BONUS CHAPTER: 21 REVOLUTIONARY STRATEGIES FOR SUCCESSFUL BABY GIRL TRAINING.

Not all potty training goes smoothly. Some children resist, preferring their diaper to the toilet. Some think the potty is toy. Some fight it every step of the way. Here is some advice on how to manage them if they rear up.

1. Starting Early

Some parents start addressing the issue with doctors at about 18 months, when they first start showing signs. Starting training at this age can be detrimental. You can purchase the potty chair and place it in the bathroom. Let them go in the bathroom when you and sit on it, but don't pressure them into go in the potty yet. Most toddlers aren't ready until at least 24 months. Give it time. It will happen.

2. Why did the Youngest Train Faster?

Families with more than one child will find that the youngest will train faster than a single child or the oldest child of the family. This is because there are more experienced potty users in the house, and this means there are more in the home to reinforce positive results.

3. Stools/Constipation

If you little one is having a hard time going, or says it hurts when he/she goes, A trip to the doctor may be warranted. Little ones get constipated as well. This leads to hard stools where it hurts for them to go. Some will have an uncomfortable look on their face as they go or look concerned before they go sit on the potty. Don't be afraid to ask them if they are having problems. You are guiding on this new phase of their life, and they need a lot of guidance.

To help avoid constipation, include some food high in fiber. If they intake about a thousand calories daily, 19 grams of fiber will keep them regular. Physical activity will also prevent constipation.

4. Reluctance to Go

They just refuse:

When toddlers learn the word "no", they like to use it, a lot. This includes telling you to know when you ask if they have to go potty. Don't worry, and don't ask too frequently. Let them tell you or show you they have to go.

If they continue to refuse, and you are at home, place a potty chair in a centralized location and let them run around with no bottoms.

Ask them if they are afraid to use the potty. Some will express fear. Just talk to them and put them at ease.

5. Don't Hover:

Don't make the process any harder than it has to be. If they don't go when you put them on the potty, don't make them sit there until something happens. This will cause a reluctance of using the potty.

When they have to go, don't hover over them and make sure they are going. Some toddlers will say they have to, sit on the potty, and nothing happens. This is normal. They are learning how to recognize the signs they have to go, and they not get it right all the time.

6. Having problems at day care:

You may find out that your child is having problems going at her daycare. This may be due to the routine the day care employees in their potty-training policies. Many day care centers take children to the bathroom in groups, often making some of the younger ones that are training be too nervous to go. After all, you have been training her to go by herself, and now she has to go potty with others at the same time. There are two ways of handling this:

Talk to the day care employees. They may be able to modify the routine so that your little one will stop having problems.

In the meantime, when you're running errands, take him/her into a public potty and explain to them that it's perfectly normal to go potty with others. This will help them become comfortable going in public and when the day care employees take a group to the potty.

Has reverted to some degree:

Routine is everything when you're potty training. If you change homes, day care, or even start going to the store on a different day may cause anxiety in the little one, making them revert to some degree. Children at this age are very sensitive to changes, problems, and marital strife, like arguing. All these things can make your little one reverts and wet themselves.

Start a reward system. Make a calendar and place a start on it whenever they go. Toys you think they will like and reward them with one when they go. Don't reward a successful potty run with food or sweets. This will cause problems in the future.

7. Won't Stop Playing to Go:

This is a common problem with toddlers just starting their potty-training routine. The use of a timer or potty watch will let them know that it is time to stop what they are doing and go to the bathroom.

A potty watch is idea for a child who is still very active and does not stay in one place playing for a while.

A timer can be effective if the child sits in one place for a prolonged amount of time. When the timer goes off, politely remind them that it is time to go to the potty.

8. Plays with their poop:

This may be somewhat disturbing to you, but they are still exploring their world. Don't yell at them if you see them do this. Calmly explain to them that the things that go in diapers, pull-ups, and the potty are not toys and they don't need to play with them.

There may also be an anxiety cause for this as well. If you suspect this is the case, again, go to your child's pediatrician. Let them know your concerns and they can help you get past this.

9. Wetting the bed

Some children wet the bed until they are in their teens, maybe once or twice a week. This is normal and may stem from being a heavy sleeper.

If they wet more than once or twice a week, there may be a deeper, both physical or psychological, issue and it needs to be addressed by a physician.

10. No more Diapers.

Once you've upgraded to pull-ups or underwear, let your care giver know that you will no longer have needed them to put a diaper on your child. This will confuse him, making it more difficult to potty train her properly.

11. Tools for Training

There are a lot more product out there to help you train your child. Here are a few of the many.

Potty Chairs:

This is small little potty seat with a splash-proof rim. This is just the right size for a toddler to sit and use the potty. The bowl removes easily so you can put it in the toilet.

Potty Seat:

This is a seat that fits snuggly on the toilet, allowing the toddler to sit on the toilet to use it. Some have bowls so you can see if they went. These bowls are removable for disposal.

Step Stool:

This is a child-sized stool that can be placed at the toilet so they can climb up and use the toilet.

Buying all three can be a little pricey in the long run. There are products out there that convert into each of the three items above, so it grows when they do, following them at each stage.

Travel Potty:

If you travel a lot, this will be an indispensable training tool. It fits on any toilet and folds for travel. There are, any different types of travel potties on the market, so finding one that suits your needs and convenience shouldn't be a chore.

12. Pull-ups

These are disposable training pants made by diaper companies to help with the training programs. They are designed to hold accidents and warn them when they need to go by allowing them to feel the moisture.

Training Pants:

If you want something that feels a little more like underwear, washable training pants will be what you are looking for to train your child. They come in many sizes, shapes, and styles.

Potty Dolls:

These training tools are to help your little better understand how to start their potty training. They come with an anatomically correct doll, a potty, and a reading material on potty training.

Potty Watches:

If you want your child to learn to stop what they're doing and potty on their own, you are going to need to pick up a potty wash. Depending on their potty habits, this watch can be set for thirty (30), sixty (60), and ninety (90) minutes. It is a countdown timer that lights up, and chimes to let the child know they need to go potty.

Potty Training Charts:

These charts are a complete rewards system for your little one. It contains stickers, charts, a reading material for training, and a keepsake certificate for when they are finished with their training. Once they have gotten three stickers on the chart, they get a reward, a toy, trip to the park, etc.

13. Don't pressure them

Even though they might show signs early, that doesn't mean its time.

Don't sit them on the potty and don't let them off until they go.

This will make them be reluctant and not want to go.

It will cause them to hold it, and fight when it's time to go.

14. Don't reward them with sweet treats.

This will start a bad precedent and cause bad eating habits.

It will tie food to good actions, causing the child to do other things to get rewarded with treats of this nature.

Find what your little one likes the most, toys, reading materials with pictures, or other things that can be used for currency.

15. Come up with a little poop song.

We all have to poo. Make it fun to poop buy coming up with a song to help them push while they pass a stool.

16. Be observant.

Your little one will give you hints and cues.

Knowing when they have to go will help them to recognize when they have to go, making training easier and more effective.

17. Don't get mad at setbacks.

They will happen.

Handle each one with patience, grace, and understanding.

Let them know accidents happen and that it's alright.

18. Coordinate with your care givers

Make sure you are all on the same page when it comes to training your child.

This will insure your little one will always be comfortable going potty.

19. Make it a big deal when they go.

Congratulate them when they go on their own.

It will make them have a sense of pride.

It will make it easier to train them, wanting them to make you proud.

20. Don't shrug them off.

We're all busy, but we can't ever be too busy to pay attention when they are trying to tell us they have to go.

21. Keep in touch with your pediatrician

Let her know during check-ups how your little one is doing with her training.

Tell them your concerns if they are being reluctant or having problems going.

Work with your pediatrician to resolve behavioral issues to make the process smoother for you and your child.

CONCLUSION

Sugar and spice and everything complicated, that's what little girls are made of. When it comes to pee training, girls are, in general, more emotionally mature, more physically mature, and have the added advantage of wearing cute, frilly training pants. But they also come with one unique challenge: wiping. Sure, you place them on the pot and let it flow, let it flow, let it flow. But unlike boys, you then have to teach their tiny little hands how to dry themselves off. And it isn't an easy feat.

First of all, there's the whole front to back issue. For as you've no doubt been taught by your mother, you want the motion of the wipe to go from north to south so that no fecal matter is introduced to the vaginal area: "Nice to meet you, Fecal Matter." "It's a pleasure, I'm sure, Vaginal Area." Because the result of this union could be a nasty and unwanted urinary tract infection.

Then, you'll need to teach your little powder puff how to determine the proper amount of toilet paper to use. Some little girls attempt the one-square-of-tissue wipe, which is, in essence, a hand wipe—yuck. Others like to ball up to half the roll of toilet paper and leave you with a clogged toilet and another item to put on your endless grocery list. Still others, like my own little princess, can't wipe themselves at all because they've pulled down all the tissue from the roll to watch it form a soft billowy pile on the floor.

Once you do devise a way to teach your girl how to get an accurate method of TP measurement, you then need to teach her the all-important scrunching of the paper itself. Some sweethearts ball the tissue so tight that it's like wiping themselves with a rock. The report needs to have the right amount of fluff, or that delicate skin can get scraped, and then ouch, there goes the potty training altogether. Others don't ball at all but just run the toilet paper close to the wet area somewhere between the legs and the water itself, forgoing the wipe all together. What you need to do is explain the "soft touch." They're not scrubbing pots and pans, at least not yet. The bottom line is that wiping is a fragile balance of many factors, all to be refined and mastered over time with lots of practice. Just make sure there's a plunger handy, lots of handwashing, and plenty of bulk-sized packages of toilet paper stored in your garage.

Another wiping concern that comes into play whenever your little passionflower graduates to the big potty (assuming that she didn't start that way) is that it may be difficult for her to balance herself on top of the toilet with one hand clutching the seat. In contrast, the other hand pulls off enough toilet paper, scrunches it up, and wipes herself dry. The chances are that she'll need both hands for these tricky tasks, resulting in fear of falling in. If this is the case, then either follow yourself a toilet seat adapter to make her feel more secure or, if you're at some toilet away from home, have your daughter get off the bathroom after she pees, then start the wiping process with her two feet planted solidly on the ground. Sure, she may get a little drizzle drippage that runs down her legs, but keep in mind, urine is sterile. Just give it a quick wipe, and all will be fine.

There's one other concern that may come into play when trying to housebreak a female. There are inevitably a few little girls who want to try peeing standing up. After all, she saw Daddy do it, and big brother, and it looked like so much fun. If it happens, don't make a big deal out of it. Explain that girls, even Mommy, need to sit down to pee. Let her watch you a few times if she hasn't already (yeah, right). Then, if she still insists on giving it a go, let her go for it. Chances are, the utter discomfort of having warm urine run down her leg, wet shoes, and socks, and the ensuing embarrassment (and teasing from big brother) will be enough to curb any more enthusiasm.

If you're feeling overwhelmed or discouraged, let me leave you with this thought: There is nothing cuter in this world than your baby girl sitting on the potty, making tinkle, balling up the toilet paper, and wiping herself. Your heart will grow three sizes at sight out of pure instinct. Who knows why? Perhaps it's a just bone Mother Nature throws us to keep up our morale as we head into training for number two.

Printed in Great Britain
by Amazon